Cambridge Elements

Elements in the Economics of Emerging Markets
edited by
Bruno S. Sergi
Harvard University

EMBRACING THE CIRCULAR ECONOMY IN DEVELOPING NATIONS

A Pathway to Sustainable Growth and Resilience

Sandeep Goyal
LM Thapar School of Management, Thapar Institute of Engineering & Technology, Patiala

Bruno S. Sergi
Harvard University and the University of Messina

Sarthak Kaushish
LM Thapar School of Management, Thapar Institute of Engineering & Technology, Patiala

Priyanka Chaudhry
D.A.V College, Ambala

CAMBRIDGE
UNIVERSITY PRESS

CAMBRIDGE UNIVERSITY PRESS

Shaftesbury Road, Cambridge CB2 8EA, United Kingdom

One Liberty Plaza, 20th Floor, New York, NY 10006, USA

477 Williamstown Road, Port Melbourne, VIC 3207, Australia

314–321, 3rd Floor, Plot 3, Splendor Forum, Jasola District Centre, New Delhi – 110025, India

Cambridge University Press is part of Cambridge University Press & Assessment, a department of the University of Cambridge.

We share the University's mission to contribute to society through the pursuit of education, learning and research at the highest international levels of excellence.

www.cambridge.org
Information on this title: www.cambridge.org/9781009705714

DOI: 10.1017/9781009705721

When citing this work, please include a reference to the DOI 10.1017/9781009705721

First published 2026

A catalogue record for this publication is available from the British Library

A Cataloging-in-Publication data record for this Element is available from the Library of Congress

ISBN 978-1-009-70571-4 Hardback
ISBN 978-1-009-70570-7 Paperback
ISSN 2631-8598 (online)
ISSN 2631-858X (print)

Embracing the Circular Economy in Developing Nations

A Pathway to Sustainable Growth and Resilience

Elements in the Economics of Emerging Markets

DOI: 10.1017/9781009705721
First published online: May 2026

Sandeep Goyal
LM Thapar School of Management, Thapar Institute of Engineering & Technology, Patiala

Bruno S. Sergi
Harvard University and the University of Messina

Sarthak Kaushish
LM Thapar School of Management, Thapar Institute of Engineering & Technology, Patiala

Priyanka Chaudhry
D.A.V College, Ambala

Author for correspondence: Sandeep Goyal, Sandeep.goyal@thapar.edu

Abstract: Many developing countries are recognizing that the traditional "take–make–dispose" model of growth is no longer sustainable. This Element explores that turning point and examines how the circular economy can offer a better path. A circular economy focuses on using resources for longer, reducing waste, and reusing or recycling materials. It offers a way to grow that can generate income, protect nature, and include more people in development. The element traces how circular economy ideas have evolved over the past decade, moving from a mainly global conversation to one increasingly shaped by local needs and realities. It argues that meaningful progress happens when three forces align: effective public policy, active communities, and strong cross-sector partnerships. Through case studies of businesses in developing countries, the Element shows how firms with limited resources use creativity to redesign products and processes, turn waste into value, and collaborate to overcome constraints.

Keywords: circular economy, sustainability, developing economies, qualitative multicase-based approach, resource efficiency

ISBNs: 9781009705714 (HB), 9781009705707 (PB), 9781009705721 (OC)
ISSNs: 2631-8598 (online), 2631-858X (print)

Contents

1 Introduction

1.1 Executive Summary

This element looks at how businesses, communities, and governments in Asia, Africa, and Latin America are rethinking growth through circular economy (CE) practices. The idea of circular economy here is not limited to recycling or using resources more efficiently. It is also about creating fairer, more inclusive, and sustainable ways of living and working. The guiding question is straightforward: how are people and organizations in developing countries turning challenges like waste, pollution, and limited resources into new opportunities for innovation and development?

The discussion is based on eleven cases from different sectors for example, e-waste recycling in India, plastic brick-making in Kenya, organic waste upcycling, and packaging and textile solutions from Latin America and Africa. These cases show how local entrepreneurs and communities are dealing with everyday problems and turning them into workable solutions. In doing so, they create businesses that are both environmentally responsible and socially relevant.

However, these efforts also face several obstacles. Many projects remain small, struggle with funding, or lack clear policy support. In many places, awareness about the importance of circular practices is also low. Together, these issues make it difficult for promising ideas to expand and bring change at a larger scale. The study suggests that one possible way forward is to start small with pilots before moving to larger regions and sectors, supported by stronger financial systems and clearer policy frameworks.

The element also sets out some lessons for managers, entrepreneurs, and policymakers, drawn from the experiences of the eleven cases. Overall, it frames the circular economy not only as an environmental strategy but also as a chance for social and economic change, rooted in local contexts but holding lessons for the wider world.

1.2 Background

There was a time, not very long ago, when Indian homes hardly created any waste. Life was simple, but nothing was casually thrown away. Each morning the milkman arrived with glass bottles. After the milk was used, the bottles were washed and kept outside for him to collect the next day. Clothes were stitched by the local tailor and then passed down from one child to another. When they became too old to wear, they turned into dusting cloths or were stitched into warm quilts filled with family memories.

In the kitchen, almost everything was used with care. Leftover food was given to cows or added to the soil in the garden. Broken radios, utensils, and other household items were not thrown out. They were taken to the nearby repair shop, where the repairman often knew each family personally. Even wedding invitations were simple and graceful, without plastic coating or glitter. People did not use big words about the environment. This way of living was simply natural, shaped by need, by habits of saving and by the quiet wisdom of earlier generations. Reusing and repairing were part of daily life and were seen as ordinary, not special.

Today many countries, especially developing ones, are struggling with fast growing waste and limited systems to manage it. In India, about 62 million tonnes of municipal solid waste are generated each year, but only around 43 million tonnes are collected and just 12 million tonnes are treated; the remaining 31 million tonnes are dumped in open sites (India Today, 2023). Worldwide, plastic production rose from 234 million tonnes in 2000 to about 460 million tonnes in 2019, while plastic waste more than doubled to 353 million tonnes. Only 9 percent of this was recycled (OECD, 2022). Global municipal solid waste reached around 2.1 billion tonnes in 2023 and may rise to 3.8 billion tonnes by 2050 if current trends continue (UNEP, 2024).

These numbers show why countries in the Global South must move from a linear to a circular economy. India's dangerous landfills such as Ghazipur in Delhi highlight this need (World Bank, 2018). Bangladesh generates about 577,000 tonnes of textile waste each year, mostly burned or dumped (Reuters, 2024). Nigeria handles nearly 500,000 tonnes of e-waste in unsafe informal conditions (UNEP, 2021). Indonesia's weak systems allow about 620,000 tonnes of plastic to enter the ocean every year (World Bank, 2020). In Kenya, over 1.6 million tonnes of sugarcane waste are mostly burned (UNEP, 2018). Ghana leaves more than 60 percent of urban waste uncollected, blocking drains and spreading disease (World Bank, 2016). The Philippines produces over 2.7 million tonnes of plastic waste a year, with around 740,000 tonnes leaking into the ocean because of single use plastics and poor recycling (World Bank, 2021).

These widespread problems show that waste is not only an environmental concern. It is also an economic and social crisis that demands urgent action. A circular economy is essential for managing waste, protecting nature and supporting fair development. It asks us to rediscover a more balanced way of living.

The circular economy offers this path. It builds on many wise practices of the past and combines them with modern tools. By reducing, reusing and recycling, it aims to keep materials in use for as long as possible, cut waste and help nature recover. As Ellen MacArthur explains, "The circular economy is not just about recycling; it's about rethinking our entire system of production and consumption, designing out waste and keeping resources in use for as long as possible."

This approach challenges the old linear model of "take make waste" that has driven unsustainable production and consumption. Instead of simply making, using and throwing away, the circular model supports refurbishing, recycling, reusing and regenerating so that resources stay in use longer.

Circularity is not only a technical solution. It also requires a deep change in mindset. Deb Caldow (2025) of Diageo notes that "One function or team alone cannot achieve circularity." It needs joint effort across companies, sectors and communities. This work explores how firms are trying to embed circularity in their daily activities in developing countries. It studies the challenges they face, the role of government support and the different factors acting at country, industry and organizational levels. It also shows how businesses are aligning their plans with the Sustainable Development Goals (SDGs), linking circularity to wider global aims.

There is strong momentum. A World Economic Forum study in 2024 reports that 75 percent of firms now see circularity as crucial, compared with 40 percent three years earlier. More than 27 percent of Nationally Determined Contributions include circular economy actions. The Ellen MacArthur Foundation's 2024 Finance Initiative SiFi Tracker shows that funding for circular projects has grown by over 70 percent in the last three years.

These trends show that the circular economy is becoming a central strategy for both businesses and governments. It reflects a growing understanding that a sustainable future needs systemic change, redesigned processes and cooperation across borders. The aim of this work is to deepen understanding of circularity and to show how businesses in developing economies are using these ideas to improve their business models. Through case studies, it highlights what is possible when entrepreneurship and innovation are directed toward circular solutions and how these examples can inspire other countries facing similar issues.

The main question explored here is how firms, communities and governments in emerging economies are adapting to and leading the shift to a circular economy, and what challenges and opportunities they encounter. To answer this, we begin with a review of existing studies to build a strong framework. We then look at new business ideas that arise within the circular economy, drawing on research to explain how entrepreneurship and innovation can support both economic and environmental goals. Finally, we present two guiding tools, the Challenge Action Framework and the EXIST Framework, which bring together our insights into clear structures to support future circular economy efforts.

2 Understanding Circular Economy: Conceptual Foundation and Research Literature

2.1 From Early Thinkers to a Structured Framework: The Journey toward Four Phases of Circularity

People often think the circular economy is a new idea, but its story began long ago. In earlier times, before factories and large industries, people lived with very limited resources. They naturally repaired, reused and repurposed what they had, not because of any theory, but because life demanded it. This was the first quiet form of circular living, even though no one gave it a name.

Things started changing with industrialization. Mass production, machines, and growing consumption slowly weakened these old habits. This was the time when economic growth became more important than care for nature, and societies moved towards a straight line of taking, making, and throwing away.

In the 1960s and 1970s, rising waste and resource shortages forced many thinkers to question this path. Walter R. Stahel became one of the key voices. He spoke about keeping products in use for as long as possible through reuse, repair, refurbishment, and recycling, so that value was not lost when something was thrown away. Other thinkers added to this journey. Some compared industries to natural ecosystems, where one process uses the waste of another. Others argued that human systems should help heal nature, not just reduce damage. Together, these ideas created today's phase of conscious circularity, where circular practices are planned and built into policies, businesses and design. In Table 1, Chronological evolution has been shown for better understanding.

2.2 Tracing Circularity Through Time: The Four Foundational Phases

The idea of the circular economy (CE) didn't just come up overnight, as was said in Section 1. Instead, it has changed over time because of how people have lived, worked, and consumed it throughout history. In this section, we have focused on the four foundational phases of circularity.

As shown in Figure 1, we identify four key phases in this evolution:

2.2.1 Phase 1: Unconscious Circularity

Long before terms like closed loop systems or regenerative design existed, many people were already living in ways that kept things in use for as long as possible. They did not think of their habits as circular or environmentally friendly. They were simply dealing with limited resources and making the most of what they had.

Table 1 Chronological evolution of circular economy concepts and theories

Stage	When/Who	Context	Concept introduced	Why it mattered	Corresponding phase
1. Traditional societies & natural cycles	Pre-industrial societies; anthropological literature	Scarcity; repair culture; reuse due to necessity.	Unintentional Circularity/ Traditional Sustainability	Life naturally operated in cycles of repair, reuse, and regeneration.	Unconscious Circularity
2. Onset of industrialization	Eighteenth to nineteenth century; early industrial economies	Mechanization, mass extraction, rising pollution.	Early efficiency thinking	Circular habits diminished as mass production became dominant.	Transition Era
3. Critique of the linear model	**1960s–1980s**: Stahel, Reday, Boulding	Waste crisis, oil shocks, economic vulnerabilities.	Closed-Loop Economy; Spaceship Earth	First structured critique of take–make–dispose systems.	Linear Economy Peak
4. Systems re-thinking in industry	**1989 onward**: Frosch & Gallopoulos; Graedel & Allenby	High industrial waste; need for interconnected systems.	Industrial Ecology	Introduced industrial symbiosis and system-level circularity.	Conscious Circularity (Early Foundations)
5. Broader systems understanding	**1990s**: Donella Meadows, Peter Senge	Climate, pollution, social issues showing interdependence.	Systems Thinking	Strengthened CE's holistic logic.	Conscious Circularity

Table 1 (cont.)

Stage	When/Who	Context	Concept introduced	Why it mattered	Corresponding phase
6. Regenerative mindset	**1994 onward**: John T. Lyle, Janine Benyus	Need for solutions that restore ecosystems.	Regenerative Design; Biomimicry	Shift from reducing harm to restoring nature.	Conscious Circularity
7. Business innovation models	**1990s–2000s**: Stahel, Lovins, Hawken	Firms needed decoupling of growth and resources.	Performance Economy; Natural Capitalism	Introduced service-based, resource-light business models.	Conscious Circularity
8. Design for circularity	**2002–2010**: McDonough & Braungart	Need for practical design frameworks.	Cradle to Cradle; Eco-Design	Provided technical and biological cycle logic.	Conscious Circularity
9. Social circularity	**2010**: Gunter Pauli; Raworth	Need for inclusive, local, zero-waste solutions.	Blue Economy; Doughnut Economics	Introduced social and ecological boundaries into CE.	Conscious Circularity
10. Formal circular economy framework	**2008–2015**: EMF, Webster	Global sustainability crisis; economic risk.	Circular Economy (structured framework)	CE becomes mainstream in business and government.	Conscious Circularity (Global)
11. Global adoption & policy integration	**2015–present**: EU, OECD, UN	Climate commitments; resource risks.	National CE Action Plans	Circularity moves to regulation and global governance.	Conscious Circularity (Advanced)

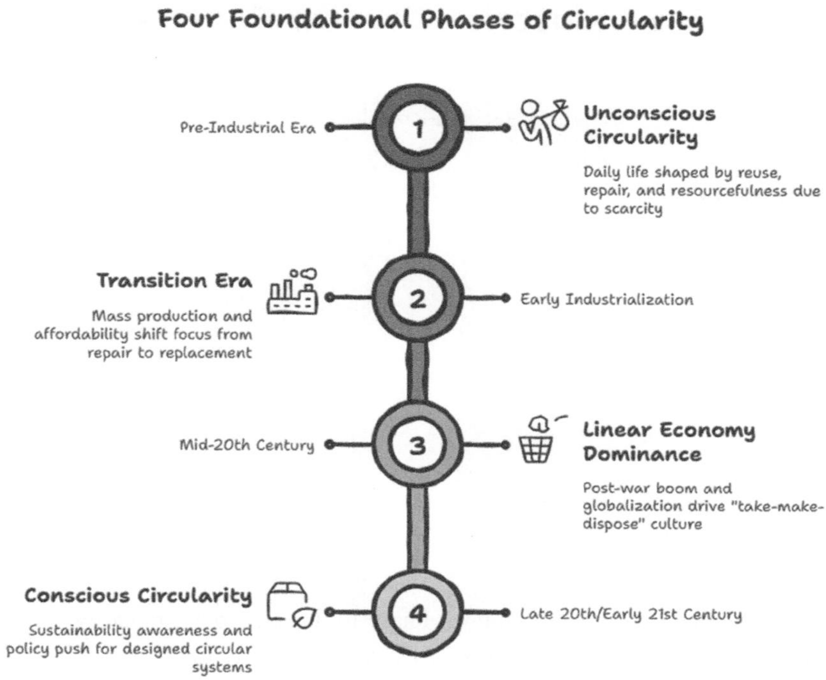

Figure 1 Four Foundational Phases of Circularity

Source: Created by the Authors using Napkin.AI (https://www.napkin.ai/)

Researchers have shown how deep these practices run in everyday life. Berkes (2008) describes how traditional societies kept materials circulating locally. Thompson (1979) explains how culture shapes decisions about what is kept, repaired, or left to decay. Cooper (2005) shows how repair and maintenance once helped products last longer. Stahel (2016) later recognized that these slow, local systems were circular long before the circular economy had a name.

In the evolution table, this everyday reality is captured as Phase 1. It laid the groundwork for later thinkers such as Stahel, Frosch and Gallopoulos, Meadows, Lyle, McDonough and Braungart, and Pauli. Their theories are more formal, but the core idea is the same, which is to keep resources in use rather than let them go to waste. Phase 1 reminds us that circularity is not new. It is something people once practised naturally, as also shown in Figure 2.

2.2.2 Phase 2: The Transition Era

As industries grew and machines became common, daily life slowly moved away from the careful use of resources that earlier generations had followed. New tools and big factories changed how things were made and how quickly

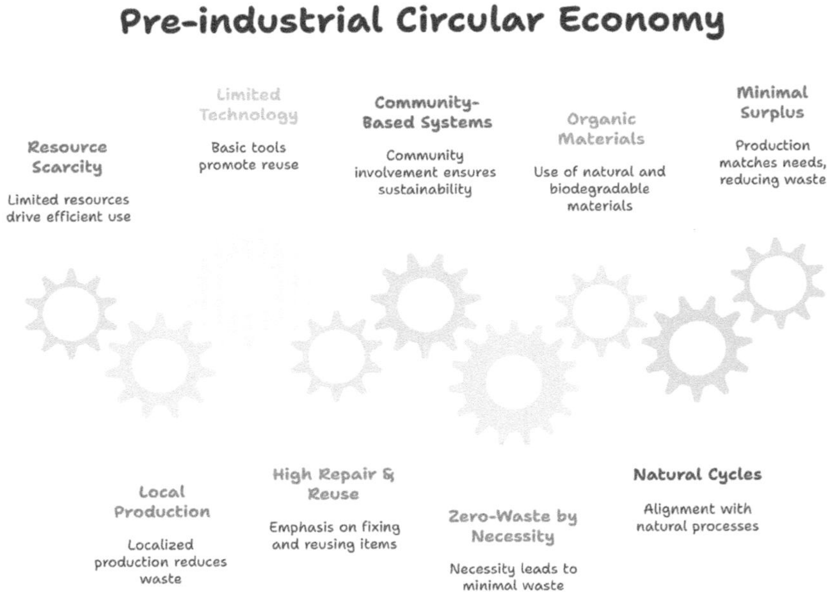

Figure 2 Circular economy – Phase 1 – unconscious circularity

Source: Created by the Authors using Napkin.AI (https://www.napkin.ai/)

they reached people. Goods were no longer made mainly by hand or from nearby materials. Companies could now take more raw materials, process them faster than ever before, and send finished products far and wide. This brought new jobs and economic growth, but it also weakened old habits of repairing, reusing, and consuming with care.

People did not stop these circular practices all at once. However, as factory made goods became cheaper and easier to buy, it began to feel simpler to throw things away and replace them instead of fixing them. Local repair and reuse slowly lost their place at the centre of daily life. Communities started to depend more on mass produced items and less on the small local cycles that once supported them.

This period was a turning point. It marked the move from a life guided by need and careful use of resources to one that valued speed, quantity, and uniform products. The benefits of innovation were clear, but the close connection between people and natural cycles quietly began to loosen. In Figure 3, we have shown the transition era.

2.2.3 Phase 3: Overexploitation and the Linear Economy

By the mid twentieth century, the world was changing very quickly. After the war, economic growth, globalization and large factories brought a flood of new

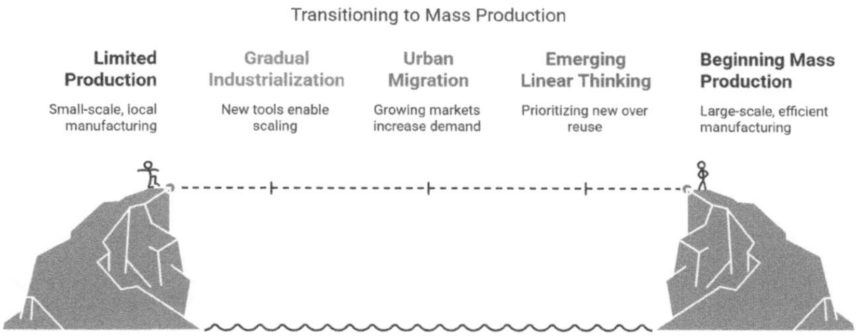

Figure 3 Circular economy – Phase 2 – transition era

Source: Created by the Author using Napkin.AI (https://www.napkin.ai/)

products into daily life. Goods could be made faster and cheaper than ever before, and owning more things began to be seen as a sign of progress. Items that earlier would be repaired and used for years were now easily replaced, and habits of care and repair started to fade.

Society moved firmly into a one way pattern of use. Industries took huge amounts of raw materials, turned them into short lived products and created growing piles of waste when these were thrown away. Researchers call this the time when the "take–make–dispose" model became deeply rooted in the economy (Kirchherr et al., 2017; Geyer, 2020). Figure 4 shows how changing lifestyles, disposable products and cheap global manufacturing all helped drive this rise in waste.

2.2.4 Phase 4: Conscious Circularity

By the late twentieth and early twenty first centuries, many societies began to seriously rethink how they used resources. Circularity was no longer just a side effect of good habits. It became a deliberate way of planning systems, shaped by concern for the environment, new government rules and the search for business opportunities.

Governments, companies, and communities started to see that care for nature could be built into products from the very beginning. Instead of simply taking materials, making products, and throwing them away, many firms explored how to keep materials in use longer, through design for durability, reuse, and recycling (Schröder & MacEwen, 2021; Tuladhar et al., 2021).With support from initiatives such as the European Commission's circular economy action plans, laws and industrial strategies began to favor more careful use of resources (European Commission, 2015b). Across many sectors, businesses tested ways

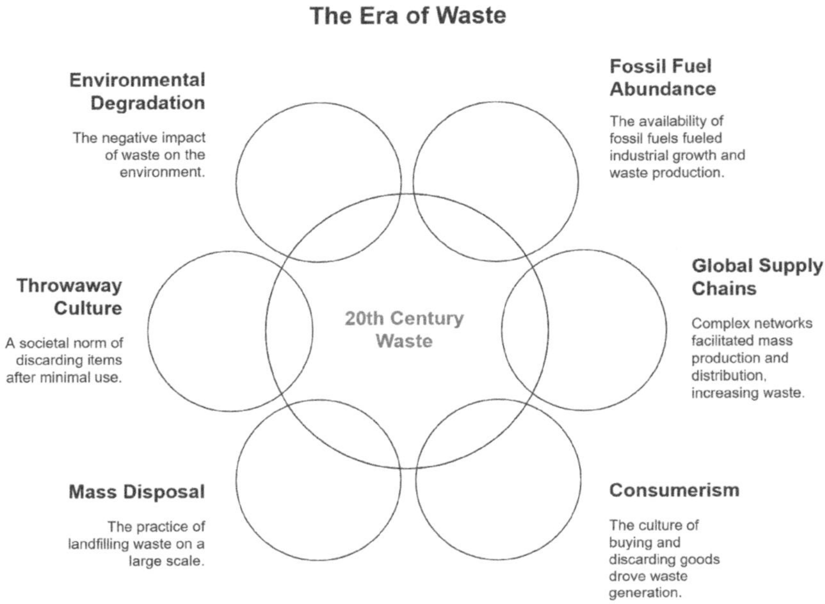

Figure 4 Circular economy – Phase 3 – overexploitation and the linear economy

Source: Created by the Author using Napkin.AI (https://www.napkin.ai/)

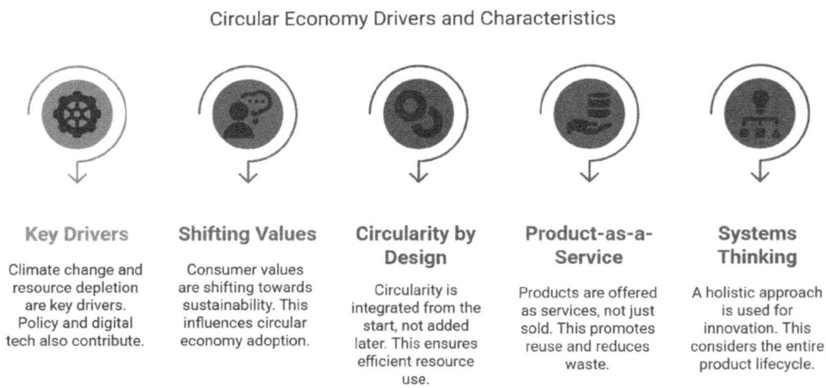

Figure 5 Circular economy – Phase 4 – conscious circularity

Source: Created by Author by using Napkin.AI (https://www.napkin.ai/)

to extend product life, repair, remanufacture, and adopt other circular practices, turning circularity into a practical business model (Bocken et al., 2019; Nosratabadi et al., 2019). In Figure 5, we have shown the circular economy drivers and characteristics in brief.

2.3 Circular Economy and Its Key Definitions

The circular economy is a broad and evolving concept, and as a result, researchers, policymakers, and institutions have defined it in many different ways. Rather than settling on a universal definition, most scholars tend to define circularity based on the specific aspect of the economy or environment they are studying.

For example, some researchers focus on the core principles of CE like reduce, reuse, and recycle while others approach it from a systems perspective, examining circularity across different levels:

- Micro level (individual products, businesses, or consumers),
- Meso level (industrial parks or supply chains),
- Macro level (cities, regions, or entire nations).

Some definitions emphasize resource efficiency, while others highlight systemic change, business model innovation, or environmental regeneration.

Because of this diversity, it becomes helpful to compare how different scholars and institutions conceptualize the circular economy. Table 2 presents some of the most influential definitions used in academic and policy literature, offering a clearer view of how this concept has been interpreted over time and across contexts.

Table 2 Key definitions of circular economy

Source/Author	**Core definition**
Stahel (1982)	*"Closed-loop economy: extension of product-life optimizes lifespan, reduces resource depletion and waste."*
Pearce and Turner (1990)	*"a new economic model based on the basic principle that 'everything is an input to something else"*
European Parliament/ EU (2015)	*"a model of production and consumption which involves sharing, leasing, reusing, repairing, refurbishing and recycling existing materials and products for as long as possible"*
Ellen MacArthur Foundation (EMF) (2015)	*"a system where materials never become waste and nature is regenerated" and is "restorative or regenerative by value and design"*
Ghisellini et al. (2016)	*"a restorative and regenerative process by design, aiming to keep products, components, and materials at their highest utility and value"*
Kirchherr et al. (2017)	*"An economic system based on business models which replace the 'end-of-life' concept with reducing,*

Table 2 (cont.)

Source/Author	Core definition
	alternatively reusing, recycling and recovering materials . . . at micro, meso and macro levels . . . to accomplish sustainable development."
Geissdoerfer et al. (2017)	*"A regenerative system in which resource use, waste, emissions and energy consumption are minimized by slowing down, closing, and narrowing material and energy loops . . . through long-lasting design, maintenance, repair, reuse, remanufacturing, refurbishing and recycling."*
Platform for Accelerating the Circular Economy (PACE) (2020)	*"one in which the value of products, materials, and resources is maintained in the economy for as long as possible, and the generation of waste is minimized."*

2.4 Descriptive Analysis

For the descriptive literature review, we used a modified PRISMA (Preferred Reporting Items for Systematic Reviews and Meta Analyses) approach to study recent work on the circular economy (CE) in business management and accounting. Focusing on articles published between 2023 and 2025, we identified key emerging themes, leading journals and leading contributing countries in this fast changing field. The review shows growing interest in how CE ideas are put into practice, how business models are designed, and how circular practices affect financial performance. Guided by the PRISMA framework, we followed a clear and structured search and selection process to keep the review transparent and easy to repeat

2.4.1 Search Strategy

The initial comprehensive search string was designed to capture a broad range of circular economy concepts: "circular economy" OR "circular business model*" OR "circular product*" OR "circular design" OR "circular supply chain*" OR "resource efficiency" OR "material efficiency" OR "waste minimization" OR "waste reduction" OR "zero waste" OR "cradle to cradle" OR "closed loop system*" OR "closed loop supply chain*" OR "remanufactur*" OR "recycl*" OR "upcycl*" OR "reuse" OR "repair economy".

Initial Documents Found: 6,59,053 (From Scopus database)

2.4.2 Eligibility Criteria and Refinement Process

The initial large dataset was systematically refined through the application of specific eligibility criteria:

- **Limitation 1: Subject Area.** The search was limited to articles on "business management" and "accounting."
  - **Documents Remaining:** 31,503
- **Limitation 2: Language and Document Type.** The search was further refined to include only "English" language and "articles" (excluding other document types like books, conference papers, etc.).
  - **Documents Remaining:** 20,259
- **Limitation 3: Publication period (Initial).** The scope was initially narrowed to articles published between 2020 and 2025."
  - **Documents Remaining:** 10,067
- **Limitation 4: Publication period (Refined) and Document Type.** The period was further restricted to "2023 to 2025," only "journal articles" were included to capture the most recent and relevant academic discourse.
  - **Documents Remaining:** 5,130
- **Limitation 5: Keyword Focus.** Finally, the keyword "Circular eco" was applied to ensure direct relevance to the core topic. This keyword likely served as an additional filter for articles primarily focusing on the circular economy.
  - **Final Documents for Review:** 1,627 (In Figure 6, we have explained the whole PRISMA process).

2.4.3 Circular Economy and Emerging Research Themes

The literature on the circular economy (CE) has moved far beyond the simple idea of "reduce, reuse, recycle." Today, it talks about changing the entire way our economy works. A closer look shows several important themes that shape both the theory of CE and the challenges of using it in real life.

One major theme is social equity. Recent research stresses that a circular economy should not only protect the environment but also be fair and inclusive. This includes creating new jobs in areas such as remanufacturing, repair, and service-based models (Stahel, 2016). It also requires investment in skills so that

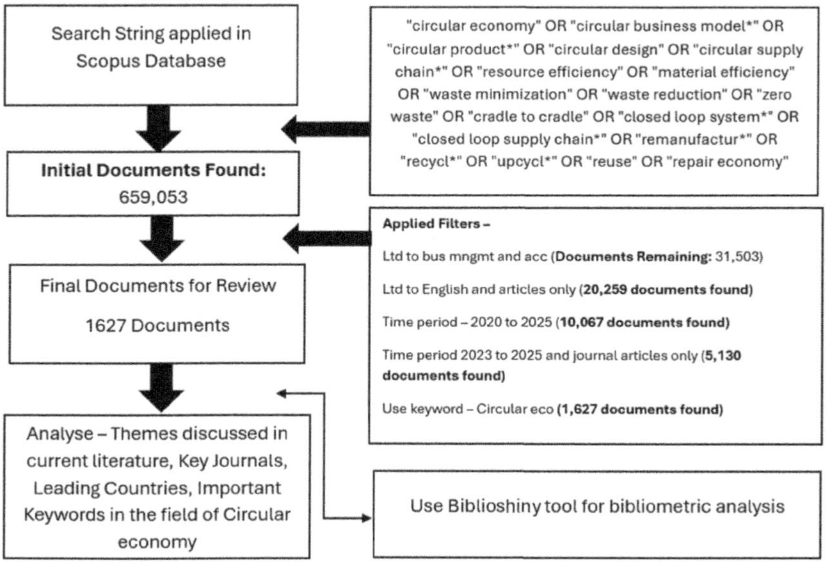

Figure 6 PRISMA approach

Source: Created by Author

workers are ready for new kinds of work. Fairness also means making sure circular products are affordable and not seen as something only for the rich (Geissdoerfer et al., 2017). Community involvement and fair working conditions are seen as essential to building socially responsible circular value chains.

Resource efficiency is another central idea. It is about using materials and energy wisely throughout a product's life. Many authors argue that it starts with design, where using fewer raw materials can greatly reduce environmental impact (Ellen MacArthur Foundation, 2015a). The focus is on getting the most value from what we already have, by making products that last longer, can be repaired, and can be upgraded (Cooper, 2005). The aim is to keep materials in use for as long as possible and reduce waste.

Because of this, product design plays a crucial role. Researchers point out that the chances for reuse, repair, and recycling are largely set at the design stage. Key ideas include designing for durability, easy repair, disassembly, recycling into good-quality materials, and modularity, where parts can be replaced or upgraded without throwing away the whole product (Vezzoli et al., 2015; Bocken et al., 2016).

Waste reduction is another important topic. Prevention comes first, followed by reuse and repair (Ghisellini et al., 2016a). Recycling and composting help turn waste into useful materials. Waste-to-energy is mentioned but is usually treated as a last option.

Business model innovation is seen as vital for applying CE at scale. Studies explore models such as product-as-a-service, leasing, renting, and the sharing economy, which encourage companies to keep ownership and care for products throughout their life (Tukker, 2015b). This is supported by closed-loop supply chains and strong reverse logistics. Finally, policy and regulation are key drivers. Governments can encourage circular practices through extended producer responsibility, waste rules, incentives, public procurement, and clear standards and certifications (Kirchherr et al., 2017).

Taken together, these elements show that CE is not just a technical fix. It involves changes in design, business, fairness, and governance. It is a full system shift, which is summarized in Figure 7.

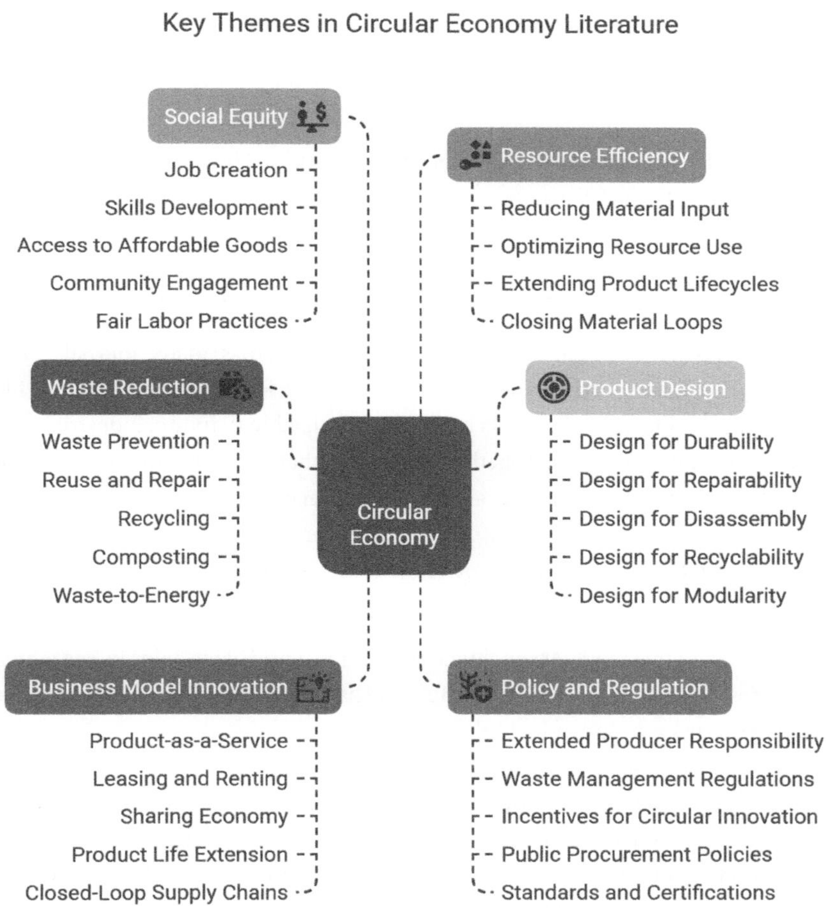

Figure 7 Key Themes in Circular Economy Literature

Source: Created by the Author by using Napkin.AI (https://www.napkin.ai/)

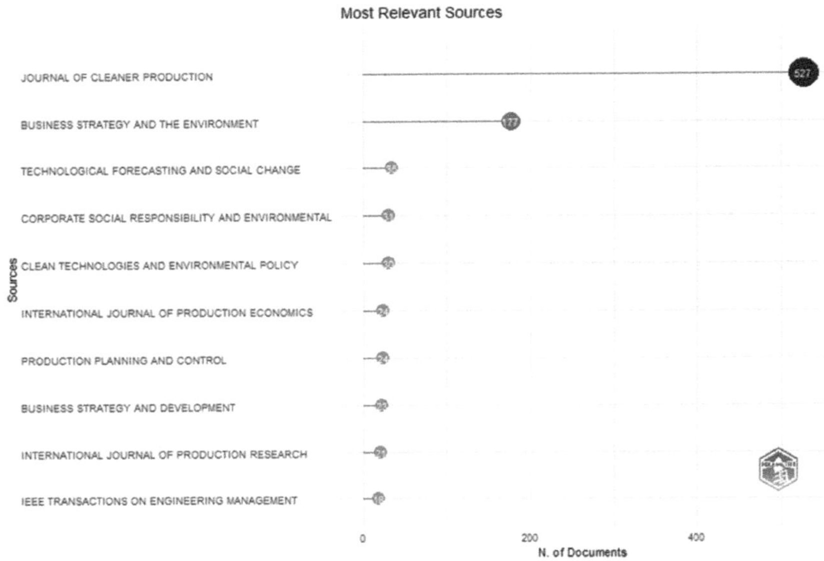

Figure 8 Top Journals by Number of Publications Through August 2025
Source: Created by the Author by using Biblioshiny (https://bit.ly/Biblioshiny)

2.4.4 Publication Hotspots in Circular Economy Literature

Research on the circular economy is published across many journals. The Journal of Cleaner Production leads, followed by Business Strategy and the Environment. Other key journals highlight social, ethical, future, industrial, and management perspectives. Together, they show that circular economy research is wide ranging. These patterns are shown in Figure 8.

2.4.5 Circular Economy Literature – Leading Countries

Our review of circular economy research also shows an interesting picture of where most of this work is being done around the world. This helps us see which countries are most active in studying and shaping ideas on circular practices. These patterns are shown in Table 3 and Figure 9.

Italy stands at the top with 725 articles, which suggests a very strong national interest and an active group of researchers working on this topic. India follows with 527 articles and China with 501. Their high numbers reflect how large and fast growing countries are turning more attention towards circular practices as they face resource pressures and set new environmental goals. The United Kingdom also has a strong presence with 470 articles, pointing to steady work in its universities and research centres. Other European countries such as Spain

Table 3 Global Research Output on Circular Economy: Country Contribution Analysis

Region	Freq
ITALY	725
INDIA	527
CHINA	501
UK	470
SPAIN	352
BRAZIL	251
AUSTRALIA	226
NETHERLANDS	199
USA	197
FRANCE	184

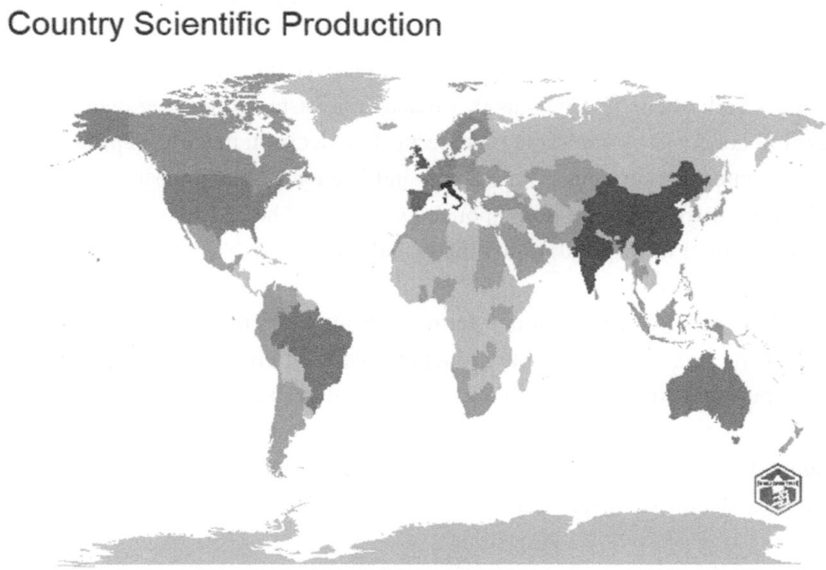

Figure 9 Global Scientific Production in Circular Economy Research
Source: Created by the Author using Biblioshiny (https://bit.ly/Biblioshiny)

with 352 articles, the Netherlands with 199 and France with 184, confirm that Europe as a whole is playing a leading role in this field, helped by supportive policies and funding.

Brazil with 251 articles and Australia with 226 show that interest is spread across different regions and economic settings. The United States has 197 articles, which is noticeable but lower than one might expect given its overall research strength. Overall, the spread of contributions shows that circular economy thinking is truly global, with Europe in front and strong support from major Asian and South American countries, all adding to the shared understanding of more sustainable ways of living and producing.

2.4.6 Keyword Landscape of Circular Economy Research

When we look at the large body of writing on the circular economy, two things become clear. One is the set of ideas that appear again and again. The other is the main themes where these ideas are studied in depth. Not surprisingly, the term circular economy appears the most, more than 1,600 times. This shows it is the main way researchers think about this subject. Close behind are words like sustainability and sustainable development. Their strong presence shows that the circular economy is seen as a path to living within the limits of nature while improving people's lives.

On the more practical side, words such as recycling and waste management appear very often. This tells us that managing waste and reusing materials are central concerns. At the same time, terms like decision making, supply chains, environmental economics, innovation and life cycle also appear many times. These point to wider questions about how we make choices, how products move from creation to disposal, how money and markets work, and how new ideas can support change.

When we link these common terms with the main themes in the literature, a clear picture emerges. Waste reduction, resource efficiency, product design, new business models, fair policies and social well-being all come together. The circular economy is therefore not a narrow topic. It combines big goals about the future of the planet with very concrete actions in many different areas. Figures 10 and 11 illustrate these patterns.

2.4.7 Mapping the Core Concepts and Research Trajectories

As we look at the research on the circular economy, two visuals help us understand the field better. One shows the main themes that shape circular economy thinking. The other shows which ideas are most important and how strongly they have been studied.

The first visual, the map of key themes in circular economy literature, highlights six main pillars. These are Social Equity, Resource Efficiency, Waste Reduction, Product Design, Business Model Innovation, and Policy

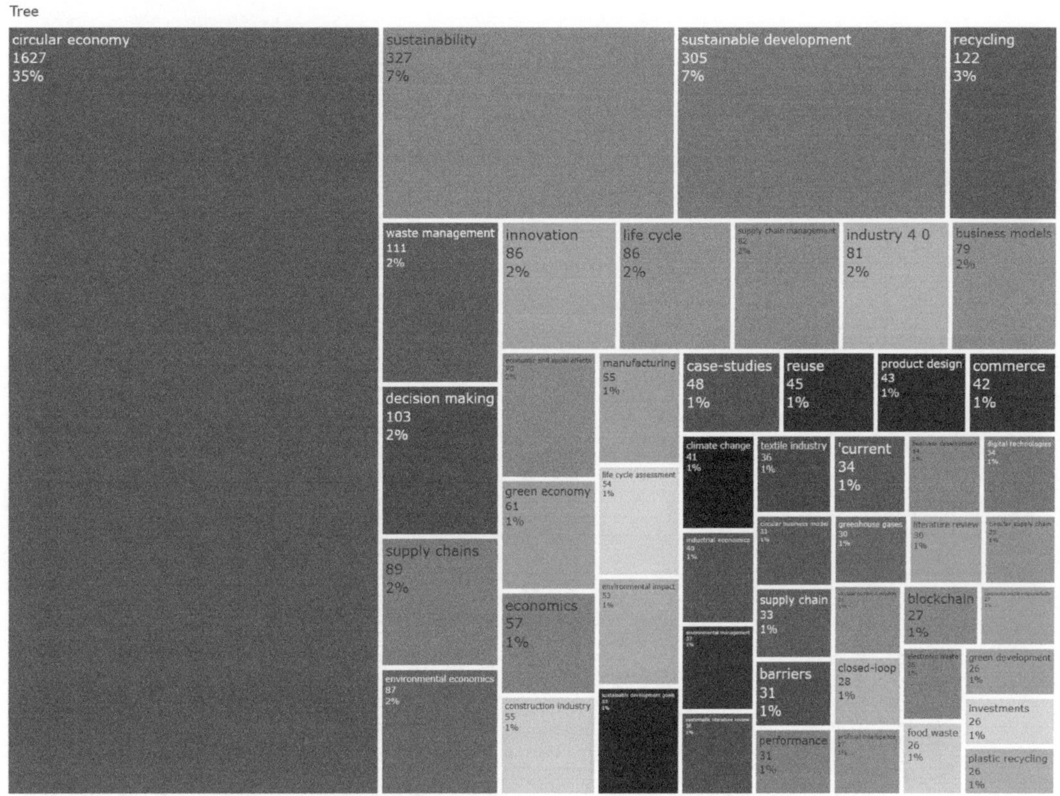

Figure 10 Keyword Landscape of Circular Economy Research

Source: Created by the Author using Biblioshiny (https://bit.ly/Biblioshiny)

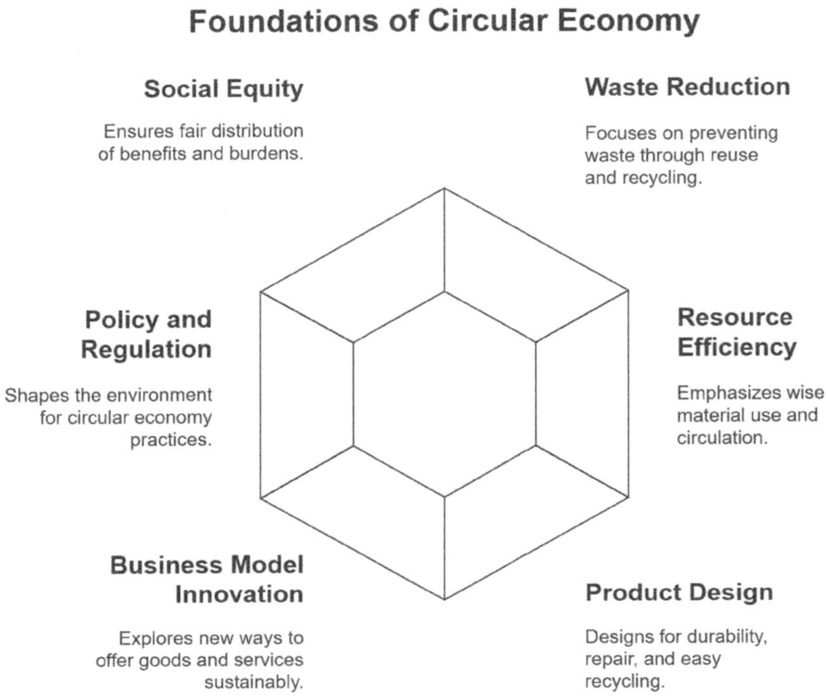

Figure 11 Connecting themes with keywords

Source: Created by Author using Napkin.AI (https://www.napkin.ai/)

and Regulation. Each theme has its own focus areas. For example, Social Equity includes ideas like job creation, and Product Design includes ideas like designing products that last longer. Together, they show how wide and rich the idea of a circular economy really is.

The second visual uses four quadrants to place research terms according to how important they are and how deeply they have been explored. In the top right corner are the strongest and most central ideas. Here we find circular economy, sustainable development, and recycling. These are the main driving forces in current research, and they strongly connect to themes like Waste Reduction and Resource Efficiency. Some broader ideas, such as sustainability or general innovation, appear less central in this specific context. However, their spirit is still present inside more focused themes like Business Model Innovation and Policy and Regulation. Together, these visuals show a field that is both wide in vision and clear about its main drivers. Please refer to Figure 12.

After looking closely at the research, it is clear that the circular economy is not a small subject. It is a large and growing area that connects many parts of our lives and work. Researchers study many things, such as how to design better

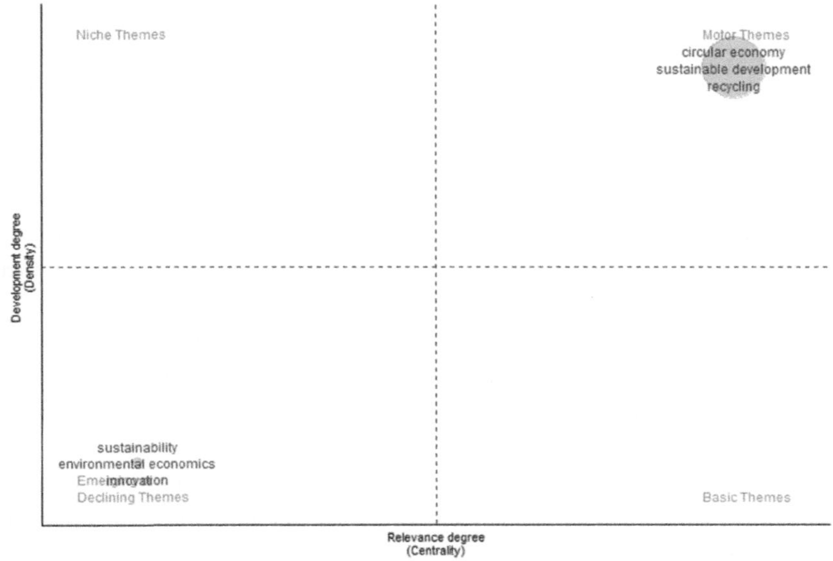

Figure 12 Trend analysis

Source: Created by the Author using Biblioshiny (https://bit.ly/Biblioshiny)

products, create new business models, make sure benefits are shared fairly and guide governments in making useful policies. Work on the circular economy is happening in many countries, including Italy, India and China. Most studies focus on ideas like the circular economy, sustainable development and recycling. This element will not try to cover everything. Instead, it will explore a few important areas in more detail.

Research Gaps and Emerging Questions

Despite growing research on the circular economy, many gaps remain, especially in the context of emerging economies. Scholars have discussed social equity, resource efficiency, product design, waste reduction, business model innovation and policy frameworks, yet we still know little about how these ideas work together in real life, particularly outside developed countries. Much of the existing work focuses on broad concepts and examples from richer nations, while local realities, cultural factors and on-the-ground challenges in developing contexts are not well understood.

Social equity is often highlighted as central to a truly sustainable circular economy (Stahel, 2016; Geissdoerfer et al., 2017). However, there is limited evidence on how circular jobs, new skills and access to affordable sustainable products actually emerge in places where informal work is common and incomes are low. In the same way, resource efficiency and product design are well developed in theory (Cooper, 2005; Vezzoli et al., 2015; Bocken et al., 2016), but we still lack clarity on how to apply these ideas widely in factories, supply chains and local industries.

Business model innovation and policy also raise unanswered questions. Concepts such as product as a service, leasing and closed loop supply chains are widely discussed (Tukker, 2015b; Kirchherr et al., 2017), yet there is little detailed research on how often they are used, how well they work and whether they can grow in developing countries. Similarly, extended producer responsibility and supportive regulation are often recommended, but we know less about how governments in emerging economies put these policies into practice and what stands in their way in terms of enforcement, compliance and public support.

Most studies still look at single parts of the circular economy in isolation. They may focus only on social, technical, economic or policy issues without fully exploring how these pieces fit together as a living system.

All these gaps show the need for research that is more holistic and sensitive to context. We need to understand how companies, communities and governments in emerging economies are actually moving towards circular practices. This leads to the core question of this element. How are different actors in emerging economies adopting and reshaping the circular economy, and what challenges and opportunities do they face in this process? By exploring this question, this element hopes to offer useful lessons for policymakers, entrepreneurs and researchers, and to show how circular principles can take root in a variety of real world settings.

3 Research Methodology, Sampling, and Data Collection

3.1 Introduction

In the previous section, we introduced the focus of this research on the circular economy (CE), particularly as it pertains to startups and companies operating in developing countries. This section outlines the research methodology employed in this study, detailing the sampling strategy and data collection techniques used to explore the dynamics and contributions of these innovative enterprises within the context of CE.

3.2 Rationale for Focus on Developing Countries

Developing countries face significant challenges in waste management and resource utilization, as reflected in the World Bank's "What a Waste 2.0" report, which indicates that over 90 percent of waste in low-income nations is inadequately managed. These regions suffer from resource scarcity, inadequate infrastructure, and increasing urban populations, rendering traditional linear economic approaches unsustainable. However, these same challenges foster grassroots creativity and frugal innovation, aligning well with the principles of the circular economy. By centering our research on these startups, we aim to uncover the remarkable opportunities for social inclusion and environmental sustainability they present.

3.3 Research Design

This study adopts a qualitative multicase study approach, which allows for a nuanced exploration of the complexities, challenges, and strategic actions taken by startups engaged in circular economy practices. The case study method is particularly advantageous for collecting and analyzing real-world data, as highlighted by Yin (2009). This research combines both deductive and inductive reasoning, employing grounded theory methods for problem formulation, data gathering, and subsequent analysis.

Deductive and Inductive Reasoning: During the initial deductive phase, a broad set of categories was established based on existing literature. These categories formed a framework that guided the subsequent inductive analysis, enabling effective organization and interpretation of qualitative data as suggested by Miles (1979).

Theoretical Sampling: A critical element of our case study approach is theoretical sampling, whereby cases are selected for their relevance to theory rather than statistical significance, following the guidelines of Glaser & Strauss (1967). This strategy includes cases that replicate previous findings, expand emerging theories, or highlight extreme examples, in line with Eisenhardt's (1989) recommendations.

3.4 Sampling Criteria & Data Collection Methods

To ensure diversity and relevance, theoretical sampling was guided by the following criteria:

Geographical Context: Startups were selected from developing countries, particularly in regions where CE practices are emerging despite infrastructure and policy challenges, such as Sub-Saharan Africa, South Asia, and Latin America. This geographic diversity allows for a comprehensive analysis of circular economy initiatives across different contexts.

Stage and Type of Enterprise: The focus was on startups and early-growth manufacturing enterprises established within the last fifteen to twenty years, driven by entrepreneurial motivations aimed at addressing waste, resource use, and environmental sustainability issues.

Circular Economy Engagement: Selected startups are actively engaged in core circular economy activities, including waste reduction, reuse, recycling, eco-friendly design, and closed-loop systems, aligning with the principles of CE.

Demonstrated Impact: Evidence of positive outcomes was a key selection criterion. This included reduced waste, lowered emissions, job creation, and community development, along with recognition from international organizations, awards, or partnerships with NGOs, development banks, or government bodies.

Sectoral and Operational Diversity: To capture a broad spectrum of practices, our sample included ventures from various industries such as agriculture, fashion, plastics, textiles, clean energy, sanitation, and packaging. This operational diversity provides a holistic view of circular economy integrations.

Data Collection Methods: The data for this research were collected through secondary data sources, including reports, organizational documents, and relevant literature.

3.5 Overview of Startup-Led Circular Innovations

Startups are playing a powerful role in reshaping how we think about waste, resources, and sustainability, especially in developing countries. This study set out to explore exactly how these early stage enterprises are contributing to circular transformations. Using a thoughtful and detailed research approach, we've aimed to capture the full picture of their impact – environmentally, socially, and economically.

Table 4 and Figure 13 offer a snapshot of eleven standout startups that were selected based on specific criteria. These companies are not only innovative, but also deeply committed to circular economy principles. They work across a range of sectors from flower waste upcycling at India's Phool.co, to textile recycling at Chile's Ecocitex, to bio-based packaging led by Craste in India. What ties them all together is their ability to turn challenges into opportunities. They're helping to reduce reliance on virgin materials, keep waste out of landfills, and create inclusive jobs for marginalized groups. These aren't just future aspirations; each enterprise is already making measurable change.

To reflect the diversity of real-world contexts, we've included companies from across the globe: Asia (India, Philippines), Africa (Kenya, Tanzania,

Table 4 Overview of selected circular economy startups from developing countries

S. no.	Company	City & country	Focus area	Circular action	How they close the loop
1	Phool (2017)	Kanpur, India	Flowercycling, biomaterials	♻ Recycling + ▲♻ Upcycling	Converts temple flower waste into high-value products like **Fleather** (leather alternative); also makes incense/compost from the same waste.
2	Attero (2008)	Noida, India	E-waste and Lithium-ion Battery Recycling	♻ Recycling	Industrial **e-waste & battery** recycler extracting metals (lithium, cobalt, etc.).
3	Craste (2018)	Pune, India	Sustainable packaging, agritech	♻ Recycling + ▲♻ Upcycling	Turns agricultural residue (stubble) into **packaging & particle boards** – value-added use of waste biomass.
4	FortunaCools (2018)	Quezon, Philippines	Cold chain + food preservation	♻ Recycling + ▲♻ Upcycling	Uses discarded **coconut husk fiber** as natural insulation for coolers, replacing plastic foam.
5	Algramo (2013)	Santiago, Chile	Circular packaging, food access	🔁 Reuse	Refill-on-the-go system that reuses durable packaging to cut single-use plastic.
6	Ecocitex (2020)	Santiago, Chile	Circular textiles	♻ Recycling + ▲♻ Upcycling	**Recovers fiber from textile waste** to spin yarn and make new garments; selects/repurposes some items.

Table 4 (cont.)

S. no.	Company	City & country	Focus area	Circular action	How they close the loop
7	Africa Collect Textiles (2013)	Nairobi, Kenya	Circular textiles	🔁 Reuse + ♻ Recycle + ▲ ♻ Upcycling	Collects/sorts used clothing for **redistribution (reuse)**; **upcycles** non-wearables into new products; builds local circular systems.
8	Salubata (2020)	Lagos, Nigeria	Footwear & fashion sustainability	♻ Recycling + ▲ ♻ Upcycling	Makes modular shoes from **recycled plastic** (post-consumer PET) → higher-value product.
9	Gjenge Makers (2017)	Nairobi, Kenya	Green construction	♻ Recycling + ▲ ♻ Upcycling	Converts **plastic waste + sand** into durable paving blocks – value-added construction material.
10	Releaf Paper (2021)	Lagos, Nigeria	Sustainable paper	♻ Recycling + ▲ ♻ Upcycling	Makes paper from **fallen leaves/green waste** – valorizing a waste stream into pulp/paper.
11	Cupfee (2014)	Sofia, Bulgaria	Eatable Coffee Cups	▲ ♻ Upcycling	**Edible/compostable wafer cups** made from cereal flours; not made from waste feedstock.

Figure 13 Location Overview of the Selected Companies

Source: Created by Authors using Google Maps (https://www.google.com/maps/d/edit?mid=1VF-iaEOCHxN5efLqVIxxquwMxgJYrFU&ll=21.97730414537169%2C0&z=2)

Nigeria), Latin America (Chile, Mexico), and Europe (Bulgaria). This geographical range allows us to explore not just common themes, but also the unique local barriers and creative responses that shape circular solutions around the world.

Together, these companies offer more than business models they represent hope, innovation, and practical pathways toward a more sustainable and inclusive future.

4 Business Cases: Overview

4.1 Phool

My journey with Phool has taught me that even waste can be beautiful, if only we are willing to see the potential in it.

— *Ankit Agarwal* (Our Better World, 2021)

Overview

Phool.co is a sustainable startup founded in July 2017 by two engineering graduates, Ankit Agarwal and Prateek Agarwal (Chowdhary, 2020). The company addresses the pressing issue of floral waste dumping by recycling temple flowers using its innovative flowercycling technology to create a variety of eco-friendly products. Phool.co also targets the critical problem of water pollution, particularly in the Ganga River, which receives an estimated 8 million metric tonnes of floral waste each year (Times of India, 2021). The startup claims to offer "the world's first profitable solution" to the temple waste crisis through flowercycling. Women employed by Phool.co collect floral waste daily from temples, which is then upcycled into organic fertilizers, natural incense, and biodegradable packaging materials (UNFCCC, n.d.).

What began as a concern for the environment has now grown into a movement that empowers communities, especially women, while giving discarded flowers a second life with purpose and dignity. Figure 14 provides a quick reference to the business overview of Phool Company.

Need Addressed

The Ganga is very important to Indian culture, but it is also very polluted, which puts the health and livelihoods of millions at risk. Phool.Co has come up with new flower cycling technology that turns these old flowers into eco-friendly items including organic incense sticks, Florafoam, and Fleather, which is a substitute for leather. Phool works on a circular economy concept and serves both businesses and consumers. It turns trash into useful things like vermicompost and biodegradable packaging. The R&D department at Phool is where the company's heart is. There, dedicated entrepreneurs work on making things that will make a difference, not just making money.

Mission

To repurpose floral waste from temples into eco-friendly products, empowering marginalized communities and preserving the environment through innovative, research-driven solutions.

PHOOL: The Circular Economy Model

Phool.co (2017)
Leading organisation: Kanpur Flowercycling Private Limited
Outreach: India
Issue Addressed: Environmental Pollution (land and water) due to floral waste dumping. The issue was addressed by recycling the floral waste into sustainable user-friendly products

Mission : "To repurpose floral waste from temples into eco-friendly products, empowering marginalized communities and preserving the environment through innovative, research-driven solutions."

Technology : Flowercycling® (Innovative process of converting floral waste from temples into eco-friendly products)

Business Model: Circular economy model (B2B and B2C)

Value Proposition: Incense sticks (DIY Incense sticks, incense cones, and flower grow kits) and Fashion Industry and Packaging Material for Products (Vegan leather goods made from flowers called Fleather, packaging material called 'Florafoam')

Revenue Streams: Direct product sales (incense, Fleather) , B2B licensing (Fleather material), Grant and award funding (e.g. UN, Earthshot

SDGs Addressed: (SDG5*, SDG6*, SDG9*,SDG11*, SDG12*, SDG13*

Socia-Economic Outcomes:
Environmental outcomes [From Inception till Year 2023]:
- ✓ 11,060 metric tonnes of temple-waste has been flowercycled® to date;
- ✓ 110 metric tonnes of chemical pesticides that enter the river through temple waste have been offset;

Social Outcomes [From Inception till Year 2023]:
- ✓ 1260 Women uplifted by Phool through sustainable livelihoods
- ✓ 356 poor families have been impacted by Phool through increased life standards and stable incomes

Overview

Phool is a sustainable biomaterial startup founded in 2017 by Ankit Agarwal in Kanpur, Uttar Pradesh, India. The company addresses the critical issue of water pollution, particularly in the Ganga River, which is heavily contaminated with around 8 million metric tonnes of waste flowers each year. Their products are handcrafted by women from vulnerable backgrounds who collect flowers from temples, empowering them while tackling the waste crisis. Phool.co not only restores the health of the river but also uplifts communities, embodying a holistic vision of environmental and social purification.

Key Stakeholders: Marginalised women and families at the base of the pyramid. People managing religious places and social gathering such as churches, gurudwaras, temples, marriages, banquet halls and birthday events; NGOs and Women self help groups, IIT Kanpur (incubation and tech), Ethical brands and designers; Sustainability forums (e.g. UN, Earthshot Prize); Investors and Grant providers

Challenges:
1) Lack of awareness and sensitivity regarding adverse impact of floral waste on marine life and soli pollution
2) Skepticism around upcycling flowers into usable products
3) Lack of Financial and mentoring ecosystem from social enterprise start-up
4) Lack of resources willing to engage with social enterprise start-up
5) Logistical challenges in procuring the floral waste
6) Lack of established process or technique for conversion of floral waste into hygienic and chemical free products
7) Ensuring consistent hygiene and quality in products made from floral waste

Key Success Factors:
1) Launched targeted campaigns to educate communities and stakeholders about the environmental harm caused by floral waste.
2) Demonstrated proof of concept through successful product lines (e.g., incense sticks, Fleather) and strong brand storytelling
3) Secured support from incubators like IIT Kanpur and later attracted global recognition and funding (e.g. UN, H&M Foundation)
4) Built a purpose-driven culture and offered dignified employment with stable income, particularly to marginalized communities
5) Developed a structured flower collection network by partnering with temples and setting up daily pickup systems
6) Invested in in-house R&D and collaborated with IIT Kanpur to innovate proprietary, safe and sustainable production methods
7) Introduced standardized quality control processes, regular training and clean production environments.

Source: Phool.co Official Website; UNFCCC, *Momentum for Change: Women for Results*, https://unfccc.int/climate-action/momentum-for-change/women-for-results/phool
* *SDG 5:* Gender Equality; SDG 6: Clean Water and Sanitation; SDG 9: Industry, Innovation, and Infrastructure; SDG 11: Sustainable Cities and Communities; SDG 12: Responsible Consumption and Production; SDG 13: Climate Action

Figure 14 Profile of Phool: Key Highlights

Source: Created by Author

Where It All Began: The Journey of Phool.co

Two friends, a festival, and a question started the story of Phool.co on the banks of the Ganges. Ankit Agarwal and an old friend went to the river to celebrate Makar Sankranti in January 2015. They were worried as they witnessed individuals gather the holy water and even drink it. The river, which was so holy and respected, was evidently dirty. Alongside the faithful, there was trash from tanneries, sewers, and factories. But it wasn't just the industrial garbage that shocked them the most. The flowers were the reason. There were a lot of marigolds, roses, and lotuses that used to be gorgeous that were now rotting in the water with chemicals and sewage. Those holy gifts were making things worse. That picture stuck with them.

"Why are we polluting what we worship?" they asked themselves. And that single question became the seed of something bigger.

Over the next year and a half, they dived deep into research – talking to priests, scientists, environmentalists, and locals. What if these flowers could be saved from ending up in the river? What if they could be repurposed into something meaningful or something that respected the devotion they were born from?

In 2017, that question took form as a company: **Phool.co.** But this wasn't just a business idea it was a mission. Ankit and his team didn't just want to clean the river; they wanted to uplift people too. So, they began working with women from marginalized communities many of whom had never held a formal job before. These women became the heart of Phool.co, handcrafting incense sticks and later, a revolutionary new material called Fleather – a sustainable alternative to animal leather.

> *Through our efforts, we aim to build natural alternatives to synthetic chemical-based products by using deep-tech and research. We are perhaps India's first natural incense brand taking a digital-first approach and have a first-mover advantage as bio-leathers are barely available in India.* —Ankit Aggarwal

Under Ankit's leadership, Phool.co has grown into more than a social enterprise. It's a movement that blends science, sustainability, and social justice. A company that asks, "What if waste could heal?" and then goes out and proves that it can. Today, Phool.co is not only preserving the sanctity of the Ganges but also restoring dignity, purpose, and income to hundreds of lives, one flower at a time. In addition to the textual analysis, we provide a visual representation of the company's journey in Figure 15.

Navigating Challenges on the Path to Sustainability

Phool.co started its journey by facing a harsh truth: millions of temple flowers, often sprayed with pesticides, were dumped into rivers like the Ganga, causing

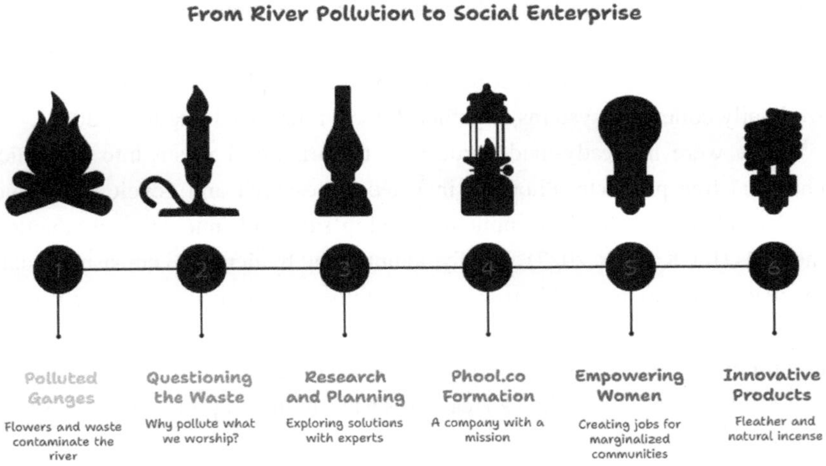

Figure 15 Journey of Phool

Source: Created by Author by using Napkin.AI (https://www.napkin.ai/)

serious harm to marine life and polluting the soil. Sadly, very few people were aware of this damage (Ramadurai, 2023). To change this, Phool.co ran special campaigns in temple communities to educate people and raise awareness about the harmful effects of floral waste.

At first, many people found it hard to accept the idea of recycling flowers used in religious rituals into new products. It was not just a practical issue but also a sensitive cultural one. Convincing people that sacred flowers could be upcycled was a challenge (The Print, 2023). Phool.co responded carefully by sharing stories that respected traditions while promoting their eco-friendly mission. They tried to explain by using proper logic such as

> *Tera tujhko arpan*. —Ankit Aggarwal

Which means, whatever is of god's, he will get it back. They launched products like incense sticks and Fleather®, a type of vegan leather made from flowers, to show how old customs and sustainability can go hand in hand.

Finding financial support was another big hurdle. Social enterprises like Phool.co often struggle to get funding and mentorship. However, support from IIT Kanpur's incubator program and recognition from global organizations such as the UNFCCC and H&M Foundation helped Phool.co grow beyond these challenges (UNFCCC, 2021; IIT Kanpur, 2022).

Hiring workers, especially from marginalized backgrounds, was also tough. Phool.co chose to focus on empowering women from communities like manual scavengers by providing them with proper training, fair wages, and dignified jobs, instead of competing with mainstream employers (Ramadurai, 2023). Another operational challenge was ensuring a steady supply of floral waste. Phool.co solved this by partnering directly with temples and setting up organized daily collection systems to gather flowers reliably (Ramadurai, 2023).

There were no ready-made processes to turn floral waste into hygienic, chemical-free products. Phool.co invested in research and development and worked closely with IIT Kanpur to develop safe and innovative production methods (IIT Kanpur, 2022). Finally, maintaining hygiene and consistent quality was essential to build trust with customers. Phool.co established strict quality controls, trained its staff thoroughly, and maintained clean production environments to meet these standards (UNFCCC, n.d.).

Nachiket Kuntla, Phool.co's Head of R&D, summed up the impact of small actions:

> *When an individual throws flowers into the river, [they] might think "what harm can a handful of flowers cause?" But multiply that across a billion people, and the effects become devastating.* (Ramadurai, 2023)

Through dedication and innovation, Phool.co turned these challenges into opportunities, creating not just a business but a movement that brings together environmental care, cultural respect, and community empowerment and even the CEO of Unilever has also shared his thoughts and he said -

> *I am impressed by your Phool enterpries in India which is perfect example of circular economy. Keep setting the standards for others to follow.* —**Paul Polman** Phool Website, 2019

4.2 Attero

> **Our technology includes special processes to recover metals from batteries, solar panels, and magnets, says Nitin. These innovations are helping the world move towards a circular economy – where waste is reused instead of thrown away.**
>
> **—Preethi, 2025**

Overview

Attero Recycling is India's largest e-waste and lithium-ion battery recycling company. It was founded in 2008 by brothers Rohan Gupta and Nitin Gupta, an alumnus of IIT Delhi. The company was started in response to a growing problem – India generates over 3.2 million tonnes of e-waste every year, making it the third-largest producer globally. Worryingly, around 95 percent of this waste is handled by the informal sector, which leads to serious environmental and health issues (Preethi, 2025). Figure 16 provides a quick reference to the business overview of Attero Company.

Attero: The Circular Economy Model

Attero (2017)

Leading organisation: Attero Recycling Private Limited.
Outreach: India
Issue Addressed: E-waste & Lithium-ion Battery Recycling

Mission : To lead the transition toward a circular economy by providing innovative, sustainable recycling solutions for electronic waste and lithium-ion batteries—recovering critical materials responsibly, minimizing environmental impact, and supporting a cleaner, greener future.

Technology : Urban mining technology and Proprietary hydrometallurgical and mechanical recycling technology

Business Model: Circular economy model (B2B and B2C)

Value Proposition: E-waste and battery recycling services, Urban mining and material recovery, Digital collection platforms, Regulatory compliance solutions

Revenue Streams: Recycling service fees, sale of recovered battery-grade metals, EPR compliance management, and digital platform facilitation.

SDGs Addressed: SDG6*,,SDG9*, SDG11*, SDG12*, SDG13*

Results

Environmental outcomes [From Inception till Year 2025]:

- ✓ Recovery over 98% of valuable materials from e-waste and end-of-life batteries.
- ✓ Save more than 100,000 tons of CO2 equivalent annually through rigorous operations

Social outcomes [From Inception till Year 2025]:

- ✓ Formalizes over 95% of the informal waste-collector network, offering them higher

Overview

Attero Recycling is one of India's leading clean-tech companies focused on solving the growing problem of electronic and battery waste. Using its own patented technology, Attero safely recycles everything from old smartphones to electric vehicle batteries, recovering valuable materials like lithium, cobalt, and gold. Instead of letting toxic waste end up in landfills, Attero turns it into reusable resources—helping both the environment and the economy.

Key Stakeholders

Electronics, EV, and battery manufacturers, Engineers, operators, research staff, Individuals using platforms like Selsmart to recycle, Venture capital firms and institutional backers

Challenges:

1. Very low public awareness about e-waste recycling
2. Informal sector dominated e-waste management using unsafe methods
3. Difficulties in building a national waste collection network
4. Need for advanced, efficient recycling technologies
5. Navigating complex and evolving EPR regulations
6. Safety and environmental risks in handling lithium-ion batteries
7. Low consumer participation in formal recycling

Key Success Factors:

1. Launched awareness initiatives; later introduced **Selsmart** for consumer-friendly e-waste pickup
2. Offered **formal, compliant, tech-driven recycling services** to build trust and credibility
3. Developed a **pan-India reverse logistics network** with local partnerships
4. Invested in **in-house R&D** and secured **multiple global patents**
5. Built **MetalMandi**, a digital platform to manage EPR and compliance for producers
6. Adopted **automated, secure recycling processes** with stringent safety protocols
7. Expanded **digital outreach**, improved app/platform UX for easier engagement

Source: Attero Recycling. (n.d.). *Attero Recycling: Official website*. Attero Recycling. Retrieved August 9, 2025, from https://www.attero.in
*; SDG 6: Clean Water and Sanitation; SDG 9: Industry, Innovation, and Infrastructure; SDG 11: Sustainable Cities and Communities; SDG 12: Responsible Consumption and Production; SDG 13: Climate Action

Figure 16 Profile of Attero: Key Highlights

Source: Created by Author

Attero is working to solve this problem by building sustainable solutions for e-waste management. Attero Recycling believes in the intrinsic value of objects mainly their inner worth. Where most see waste, the company sees potential: the potential for renewal and purpose. Through its process of e-cycling, Attero gives obsolete electronics a new life and a new role and helping to protect the Earth from landfills, pollution, resource depletion, and deforestation.

The company operates on the principle that the values upheld today will shape whether the twenty-first century becomes a "Century of the Environment" and whether society can truly become sustainable. Attero recognizes that we stand at a critical crossroads that is one that demands responsibility, long-term thinking, and action beyond short-term convenience.

Committed to this vision, Attero is determined to contribute to building an environmentally sound future. The company emphasizes that real change begins with individual accountability and encourages everyone to recognize their role in protecting the planet, continuously reflecting on and improving their environmental efforts

One of their main focuses is recovering valuable materials like lithium, nickel, and cobalt from discarded electronics, which can then be reused in new products. Their recycling facility in Roorkee, Uttarakhand, uses advanced technology and is supported by a nationwide logistics system and IT infrastructure that allows for complete waste tracking.

From a small startup, Attero has grown into a major player in the clean technology space. With its own patented recycling methods, a strong digital network, and plans to expand globally, the company is focused on tackling the e-waste crisis while contributing to a more sustainable, circular economy

Need Addressed – Attero Recycling Pvt. Ltd. is working to solve one of India's biggest environmental problems: how to deal with electronic garbage. A lot of e-waste in the country is now being handled through unofficial methods, which are often dangerous and cause major pollution and health problems. Attero offers a safe and organized way to recycle e-waste using cutting-edge technology to get back valuable metals like lithium, nickel, and cobalt. It does this by lowering the need for mining new resources and reducing damage to the ecosystem. The company also aims to make the informal sector more official and help it grow, in addition to recycling. Attero's digital platform MetalMandi makes e-waste trading more open and gives waste pickers more ways to make money. Selsmart is another program that makes it safe to collect e-waste and destroy data. This encourages people and businesses to get rid of their electronic waste in a responsible way. Attero is helping to build a more sustainable circular economy in India by merging new technologies with social inclusion. This economy will not only deal with the problems caused by e-waste, but it will also provide economic and social value.

Mission – Our goal is to become the best at recycling e-waste and finding the best and most environmentally friendly approach to solve the e-waste challenge.

Where It All Began: The Journey of Attero

An outdated laptop was the first thing that started Attero Recycling's tale. When co-founders Rohan Gupta and Nitin Gupta (who went to IIT Delhi) tried to get rid of their old gadget in a responsible way, they found out how hard it was to find a secure and trusted choice. What looked like a tiny problem for me turned out to be a much bigger one: India, one of the world's biggest manufacturers of electronic debris, didn't have a well-organized and environmentally friendly way to handle e-waste.

This realization was what started Attero. The two creators wanted a system that would do more than just make sure that things were thrown away safely. They sought to turn technological garbage into a chance, an unused resource. In 2008, they started Attero Recycling with the purpose of getting valuable metals including gold, silver, copper, tin, aluminum, lithium, cobalt, manganese, and nickel back from outdated devices.This method allowed things that were once thought of as "waste" to be salvaged, purified, and used again. These materials could be taken straight from outdated gadgets instead of being dug up from the ground. This is often called "urban mining." Attero wanted to shift how people in India thought about trash and sustainability by changing how they thought about e-waste from a burden to a source of value. Attero has become a leader in clean technologies throughout the years. The business uses innovative logistics and internet platforms along with eco-friendly recycling procedures. Attero's journey – from dealing with a personal problem to building a national reverse logistics network and a modern recycling facility – shows how one broken laptop led to a bigger goal: to protect the planet, create a sustainable circular economy, and reduce reliance on imported critical minerals, one device at a time. Along with the text analysis, Figure 17 shows the company's path in a visual way.

Navigating Challenges on the Path to Sustainability

Attero's journey started in 2008 when Nitin and Rohan Gupta faced a common issue: they couldn't safely dispose of their old laptop. This experience revealed a significant gap in India's e-waste management system, where safe and environmentally friendly recycling was nearly non-existent. At that time, India was generating millions of tonnes of e-waste each year, yet more than 95 percent of

Figure 17 Journey of Attero

Source: Created by Author by using Napkin.AI (https://www.napkin.ai/) and (https://attero.in)

it was managed by the informal sector. They often used hazardous methods like open-air burning, acid leaching, or illegal dumping (Wikipedia, 2025). Seeing the environmental and health risks, the founders aimed to create India's first formal e-waste recycling facility in Roorkee, Uttarakhand. However, establishing a full processing plant without any prior examples was a huge logistical, financial, and regulatory challenge.

Regulations were weak, unclear, and poorly enforced. The founders needed to work closely with policymakers while investing in compliance systems and infrastructure that anticipated future laws, well before official mandates were in place.

A major hurdle was the unregulated dominance of the informal sector, where local scrap dealers (kabadiwalas) collected and dismantled electronics using basic and often toxic methods. Rather than compete, Attero decided to collaborate. They launched MetalMandi, a digital platform that allowed scrap dealers throughout India to join the formal network. It provided standardized pricing, better handling, and financial support.

> *With MetalMandi, a dealer in Kolhapur gets the same fair price and service as someone in Delhi. That's powerful,* said Nitin Gupta (The Better India, 2025).

Another significant challenge was low consumer awareness and a lack of trust. Most people kept old devices at home or sold them informally, unaware of the risks or advantages of proper disposal. To change these habits, Attero introduced Selsmart, a direct-to-consumer platform offering: Doorstep e-waste pickup, Instant payment and Certified data destruction services to address privacy concerns

> *Consumers want transparency and trust, especially when giving away phones and laptops with personal data. That's what we built with Selsmart,* said Nitin Gupta (The Better India, 2025).

On the policy side, compliance with Extended Producer Responsibility (EPR) requirements added another layer of difficulty. Many producers were uncertain about how to meet targets, and recycling companies needed to set up systems to absorb costs and track volumes.

> *If you have to create scientific capacity for recycling, you need extra profits. This is good for us,* said Nitin Gupta about minimum pricing policies for recyclers (India Today, 2025).

Initially, funding was also a significant challenge. Investors considered e-waste recycling too costly and specialized. Attero had to demonstrate its business case by showing how environmental benefits could match profitability and the long-term demand for recovered materials. The company then faced the challenge of technology development. There were no tools available for clean and efficient recycling of batteries and circuit boards, so Attero invested in in-house R&D to create proprietary, patented technologies capable of extracting valuable materials like: Gold, silver, tin, Lithium, cobalt, nickel, manganese, and aluminum. As demand for EV batteries and essential minerals increased, Attero positioned itself as a leader in urban mining, transforming discarded electronics into a source of raw materials for the clean energy economy. Lastly, India's scale itself presented a challenge. Building a nationwide reverse logistics system to collect, track, and move e-waste required a solid digital foundation. Attero addressed this by developing IT-enabled systems for real-time tracking and regulatory compliance.

4.3 Craste

Our vision is to transform an environmental problem into a socio-economic opportunity
—Shubham Singh (Nath, 2024)

Overview

Craste, founded in 2018 by siblings Shubham Singh and Himansha Singh in Pune, is an innovative Indian startup that turns agricultural waste, like rice, millet, sugarcane, and barley, into eco-friendly products such as particle boards and sustainable packaging materials (The Indian Express, 2024). Their first manufacturing facility, located in Morena near Gwalior, has become cost-competitive, showing that their model works well (The Indian Express, 2024). Craste's mission goes beyond making products in a sustainable way; they also want to address environmental problems and economic issues in rural areas. As clearly states, (The Indian Express, 2024). Figure 18 provides a quick reference to the business overview of Craste Company.

Mission

Craste's mission is to drive a sustainable, circular economy by transforming agricultural waste – traditionally burned and wasted – into eco-friendly, high-value materials such as formaldehyde-free particle boards and biodegradable packaging. The startup aims to reduce environmental degradation, combat climate change, and simultaneously create economic opportunities for rural communities

Need Addressed

Craste addresses the urgent problem of agricultural stubble burning in India, a major contributor to severe air pollution and greenhouse gas emissions, particularly in northern states like Punjab and Haryana. Farmers often burn crop residue due to limited time, resources, and viable alternatives. At the same time, industries continue to rely on unsustainable materials like plastic, thermo-col, and formaldehyde-based particle boards, which are harmful to both health and the environment. Craste tackles both issues by converting crop waste into

Craste: The Circular Economy Model

Craste (2017)
Leading Organisation: Craste Pvt. Ltd.
Outreach: India
Issue Addressed: Agricultural Waste, Unsustainable Packaging, and Formaldehyde-Based Boards.,

Mission: To lead the transition toward a circular economy by transforming crop residues into high-value, eco-friendly products. Craste provides sustainable alternatives to plastic and wood, while reducing carbon emissions, preventing stubble burning, and supporting green innovation in packaging and construction industries.

Technology : Zero-liquid discharge pulping technology, agro-waste-to-board innovation, and formaldehyde-free engineered boards

Business Model: Circular economy model (B2B and B2C)

Value Proposition: Climate-positive packaging and furniture materials, Substitutes plastic, thermocol, and MDF/plywood, Enhances rural income through farmer engagement, Offers formaldehyde-free products for healthier indoor environments

Revenue Streams: Sale of eco-boards (B2B furniture and construction sector), Sale of sustainable packaging (food, FMCG, D2C brands), Customized packaging design and consulting

SDGs Addressed: SDG8*,,SDG11*, SDG12*, SDG13*, SDG14* SDG15*

Results

Environmental outcomes [From Inception till Year 2025]:
- ✓ Reduced ~30 kg of CO_2 emissions per eco-board produced
- ✓ Manufactured 100% biodegradable packaging to replace single-use plastics

Social outcomes [From Inception till Year 2025]:
- ✓ Pays ₹6/kg for crop waste that was previously burned (2023)
- ✓ Generates local jobs in board and packaging production units
- ✓ Engages rural women in sustainable manufacturing roles

Overview

Craste is an award-winning Indian cleantech startup that addresses the dual problem of agricultural residue burning and unsustainable industrial materials. By converting agro-waste into formaldehyde-free boards and food-grade packaging, Craste enables climate-conscious manufacturing and rural empowerment. The company operates across multiple Indian states, collaborating with farming communities and sustainable brands.

Key Stakeholders

Farmers (agricultural waste suppliers)FMCG, food, and e-commerce brands (eco-packaging buyers)Furniture and construction companies (eco-board users)Rural collection and processing partners, Government & regulatory bodies (for green procurement and compliance)Impact investors and ESG-focused VCs, Environmental advocacy groups

Challenges:

1. Farmer resistance and lack of awareness about crop waste monetization
2. Difficulty in maintaining consistent raw material supply
3. Higher production costs compared to conventional plastic or wood products
4. Convincing brands and businesses to switch from plastic/thermocol
5. Lack of formal standards and testing for alternative materials
6. Limited funding in early stages

Key Success Factors:

1. Farmer engagement programs and financial incentives
2. Developed a decentralized sourcing and collection system
3. Achieved cost competitiveness by refining manufacturing efficiency and using zero-liquid-discharge methods.
4. Focused on premium clients willing to pay for sustainable impact — e.g., D2C brands, FMCGs, and food exporters.
5. Produced food-grade packaging and formaldehyde-free boards that comply with industry and environmental norms.
6. Gained funding and mentorship from Techstars, Marico Innovation Foundation, and others, helping to scale responsibly.

***Source:** Craste. (n.d.). Craste – We Build It Better [Homepage]. Retrieved August 12, 2025, from https://craste.co/*
SDG 8:Decent Work and Economic Growth;SDG 11: Sustainable Cities and Communities; SDG 12: Responsible Consumption and Production; SDG 13: Climate Action; SDG 14: Life Below Water; SDG 15: Life on Land

Figure 18 Profile of Craste: Key Highlights

Source: Created by Author

eco-friendly packaging and formaldehyde-free boards, offering farmers an alternative income stream while reducing pollution and deforestation

Where It All Began: The Journey of Craste

The origins of Craste trace back to Shubham Singh's postgraduate studies in chemical engineering at Imperial College London. While there, he came across alarming reports about Delhi becoming one of the most polluted cities in the world. Drawing from his research on sustainable materials, he saw potential in crop waste: "Crop burning is a very big problem in India . . . For me, crop waste was an important opportunity" (The Indian Express, 2024). After returning to India in 2017 with a grant from BIRAC, he and his sister founded Craste in 2018. They had a clear vision of creating high-value, eco-friendly products while improving rural incomes through farmer involvement (The Indian Express, 2024). By establishing their first plant in Morena, Craste positioned itself close to sources of raw materials, which improved logistical efficiency. The company aims to cut carbon emissions significantly. Each 8 ft × 4 ft × 18 mm particle board they produce helps reduce approximately 30 kg of CO_2 output (The Indian Express, 2024). Building on this momentum, Craste is ambitious. They plan to run ten small factories across India, with an additional office in Bengaluru, and to increase revenue in the current fiscal year (The Indian Express, 2024). In addition to the textual analysis, we provide a visual representation of the company's journey in Figure 19.

Navigating Challenges on the Path to Sustainability

The journey wasn't straightforward. One of the first major hurdles Craste faced was convincing farmers to part with their crop waste. In India, farmers often burn stubble simply because they have no alternative. Machinery for residue removal is costly, and the time between harvesting and sowing is only 15–20 days. Craste tackled this by engaging farmers directly, paying them ₹6 per kg for the waste, and creating a decentralized sourcing model. This made it feasible to collect large volumes from scattered rural areas. "Farmers had a time window of just 15 to 20 days and burning was their easiest option. We changed that by giving value to what was once considered useless" (The Story Watch, 2023). Scaling the manufacturing process presented another challenge. Sustainable materials like Craste's were more expensive than plastic or conventional particle boards, making it hard to compete on price. Instead of targeting mass markets right away, Craste focused on ESG-conscious brands and food exporters willing to pay more for sustainability and safety. They invested heavily in research and development, coming up with proprietary, patent-pending

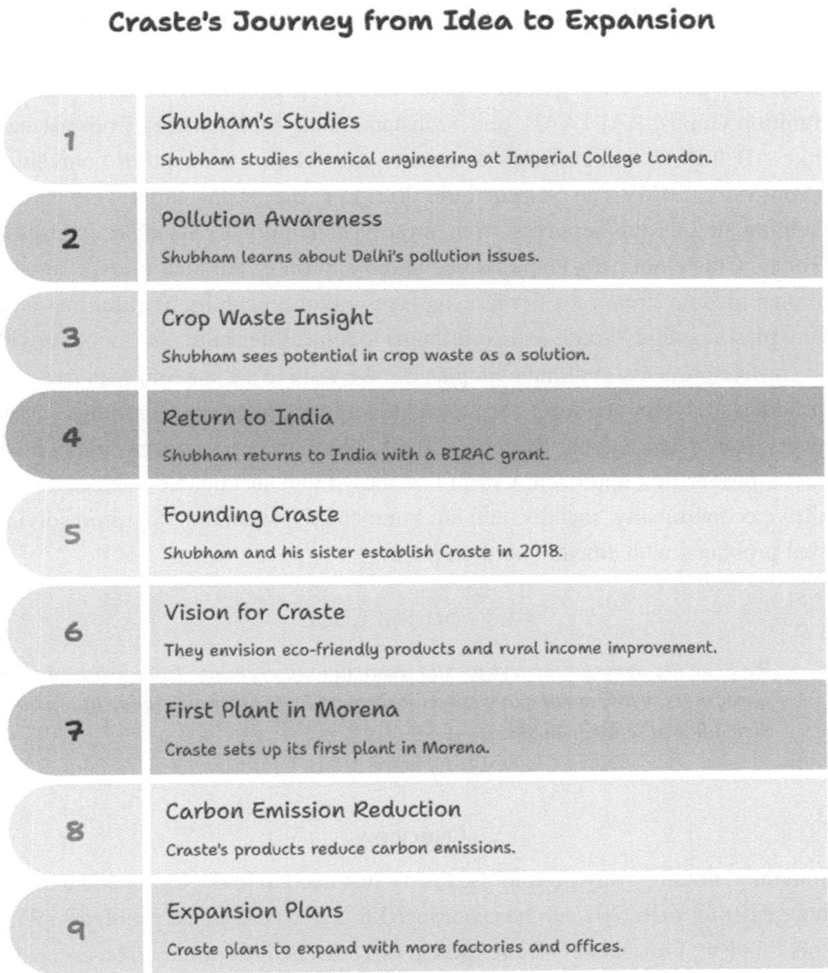

Figure 19 Journey of Craste

Source: Created by Author by using Napkin.AI (https://www.napkin.ai/)

technologies like Fumasolv – a green chemical process that extracts lignin for use in biodegradable packaging – and a formaldehyde-free adhesive for their eco-boards. This addressed both performance and health standards (The Startup Lab, 2021; Marico Innovation Foundation, 2023). Craste's COO, Dr. Himansha Singh, highlighted the company's commitment to overall impact: "Craste fosters the circular economy with benefits for farmers, the environment, and the consumer". The company set up an Agri Fibre Conversion Unit that follows zero-liquid-discharge principles, greatly reducing water use and cutting carbon emissions by about 30 kg of CO_2 for each board produced (Marico Innovation

Foundation, 2023). Another obstacle was securing early-stage funding. Like many cleantech startups, Craste initially struggled to attract investment, but they kept going. They gained support through grants from BIRAC (Biotech Ignition Grant), RAFTAAR, and Techstars, along with backing from partners like AB InBev, Stanley Black & Decker, and Marico Innovation Foundation (YourStory, 2021; The Startup Lab, 2021). These partnerships were key in helping the startup progress from prototype to pilot to scalable enterprise. Today, Craste not only helps reduce stubble burning but also creates an additional income stream for farmers, replaces environmentally harmful materials like plastic and plywood, and contributes to a healthier built environment with toxin-free products. As Shubham puts it, "We want to see a world with tree-free products . . . where we don't have to cut down living trees to make things we use every day" (Aria Global Systems, 2023). Through perseverance, innovation, and a farmer-first approach, Craste has shown that sustainable businesses can thrive economically, socially, and environmentally when they focus on solving real problems with empathy and purpose.

4.4 Fortuna Cools

> ***We hear the demand for less plastic waste among everyone from fish traders to sunbathers, while small-scale coconut farmers have no choice today but to burn their piles of leftover husks.***
>
> *David Cutler, Co-Founder & CEO, Fortuna Cools (Adams, 2021)*

Overview

In nature, nothing truly goes to waste. We just need to look closely and explore how existing materials can be repurposed to solve real-world problems. With this mindset, Fortuna Cools emerged in 2018 in the Philippines. The company aimed to improve local fish packaging practices and support rural livelihoods. Their innovation came from using coconut husks, an agricultural byproduct that farmers often discard, to create sustainable, high-performance insulation.

Founded by David Cutler and Tamara Mekler, Fortuna Cools specializes in developing eco-friendly insulated packaging solutions. Their products provide a sustainable alternative to traditional plastic foam packaging, particularly Styrofoam, by using the natural insulating properties of coconut fiber. These solutions cater mainly to cold-chain logistics, such as the transport of seafood, dairy, pharmaceuticals, and fresh produce.

Fortuna's products are not only durable and highly insulative but also competitively priced. This makes them an appealing option for businesses looking to reduce their environmental impact. The company serves a diverse customer base, including seafood and produce traders, retailers, and restaurants, especially in regions like the Philippines. There is growing momentum to phase out plastic-based packaging. Figure 20 provides a quick reference to the business overview of Fortuna Cools.

Need Addressed

Fortuna Cools addresses two major issues. First, there is the common use of non-biodegradable Styrofoam in cold storage. Second, rural farming communities often do not make good use of coconut husk waste. The company transforms discarded husks into eco-friendly insulation. This approach not only cuts down on plastic pollution but also offers a sustainable income for smallholder coconut farmers (Fortuna Cools, n.d.; Green Queen, 2021).

Where It All Began: The Journey of FortunaCools

Fortuna Cools started as a graduate school project aimed at solving a practical cold-chain issue for small-scale tuna fishermen in Southeast Asia (Fortuna Cools, n.d.). Co-founders David Cutler and Tamara Mekler spent time in fishing villages to see how perishable goods, like fish, were stored and transported. They quickly noticed that Styrofoam boxes were common, fragile, and harmful to the environment. However, alternatives were often out of reach and too expensive for small vendors (Manila Bulletin, 2024).

Using coconut husk fibers, an abundant local agricultural byproduct as a starting point, the founders experimented with replacing synthetic insulation with a biodegradable, locally sourced material. After several attempts, they created the Coconut Cooler, a strong, reusable option made from compressed coconut husk insulation panels and recycled plastic. This product was designed to keep ice frozen for up to 48 hours, matching the performance of traditional polystyrene but avoiding the waste (Ingredients Network, 2021; Manila Bulletin, 2024). Fortuna Cools officially launched in 2018, building its early supply chain on direct relationships with smallholder coconut farmers in the Bicol region and nearby rural communities (Fortuna Cools, n.d.). Their production model focused on local sourcing, simple processing, and caring for the environment. This approach helped the company stay sustainable while ensuring quality and performance.

To increase its impact and grow its operations, Fortuna Cools secured seed funding in 2021 from investors aligned with its mission, including ADB Ventures, Katapult Ocean Fund, Manila Angel Investors Network, and Pasudeco Development Corporation (Food and Drink Digital, 2021; Green Queen, 2021). This funding allowed the company to boost its manufacturing

Fortuna Cools: The Circular Economy Model

Founded: 2018
Leading Organisation: Fortuna Cools Inc.
Headquarters: Manila, Philippines (production in Bicol region)
Issue Addressed: Plastic foam insulation waste and coconut husk burning.,

Mission: Fortuna Cools wants to replace plastic foam insulation with sustainable, high-performance options made from natural coconut fiber. This change will cut down on plastic pollution and emissions. It will also provide income opportunities for small coconut farmers in the Philippines.

Technology : hydraulic pressing to compact processed coconut fiber into sturdy insulation boards, which are then assembled into coolers

Business Model: Circular economy model (**B2B sale)s** to seafood and agricultural suppliers and **B2C retail** via their consumer line (*Nutshell*).

Value Proposition: Climate-positive packaging and furniture materials, Substitutes plastic, thermocol, and MDF/plywood, Enhances rural income through farmer engagement, Offers formaldehyde-free products for healthier indoor environments

Revenue Streams: Wholesale and bulk orders for Seafood, agriculture, and cold-chain logistics sectors.Retail sales of Nutshell Cooler for consumer outdoor and grocery use.

SDGs Addressed: SDG8*,,SDG11*, SDG12*, SDG13*, SDG14* SDG15*

Results

Environmental outcomes [From Inception till Year 2025]:

- ✓ Processed over **600,000 coconut husks** into coolers and panels
- ✓ Prevents emission of CO_2 associated with husk burning and Styrofoam waste.

Social outcomes [From Inception till Year 2025]:

- As of October 2024, More than 1,000 fisher families enjoy improved livelihoods, and more than 1,200 coolers have been sold

Overview

Fortuna Cools turns coconut husks, which are often burned as agricultural waste, into strong, biodegradable coolers and cold-chain packaging. The company is based in the Philippines. It sources husks from over 250 smallholder farms every day and mixes them with recycled plastic bottles. This creates insulation panels that can keep ice frozen for up to 48 hours. Each cooler requires about 37 coconut husks and 50 recycled plastic bottles to make (Manila Bulletin, 2024).

Key Stakeholders

Smallholder coconut farmers (source of raw material)Seafood and agricultural vendors (commercial buyers)Consumers (via the Nutshell cooler)Investors such as ADB Ventures and Katapult Ocean Fund, NGO collaborators facilitating community engagement

Challenges:

1. Competition from low-cost Styrofoam
2. Environmental pollution from burning coconut husks
3. Scaling production using agricultural waste
4. Market resistance to new packaging materials
5. Need for funding and growth support

Key Success Factors:

1. Developed eco-friendly coconut husk insulation with similar performance
2. Repurposed husks into biodegradable insulation panels
3. Built rural supply chains and used hydraulic presses for manufacturing
4. Partnered with companies like Grab to validate product in real-world use
5. Secured investment from ADB Ventures and other backers

Source: Fortuna Cools. (n.d.). *Fortuna Cools: Sustainable natural fiber insulation.* Retrieved August 11, 2025, from https://www.fortunacools.com
SDG 8:Decent Work and Economic Growth; SDG 11: Sustainable Cities and Communities; SDG 12: Responsible Consumption and Production; SDG 13: Climate Action; SDG 14: Life Below Water; SDG 15: Life on Land

Figure 20 Profile of Fortuna: Key Highlights

Source: Created by Author

capabilities and introduce a consumer-friendly version of its product – the Nutshell Cooler. This cooler is collapsible, stylish, and durable, targeting retail markets and outdoor users (En-SJGLE, 2021).

Reflecting on the company's values, co-founder David Cutler said:

> *We're trying to replace as much plastic foam with natural fiber as we possibly can and benefit thousands of coconut farmers in the process (Manila Bulletin, 2024).*

Today, Fortuna Cools continues to expand its reach by balancing local economic growth with global environmental goals. They are turning an agricultural waste issue into a business opportunity that links climate action with community livelihoods. In addition to the textual analysis, we provide a visual representation of the company's journey in Figure 21.

Navigating Challenges on the Path to Sustainability

Fortuna Cools, founded in 2018, faced several key challenges in its mission to create sustainable alternatives to plastic foam packaging. One major obstacle was competing with Styrofoam, a material widely used in cold-chain logistics due to its low cost and effectiveness. Over 300,000 Styrofoam boxes are used in the Philippines' seafood trade alone, making it difficult to replace (Fortuna Cools, n.d.). To address this, Fortuna Cools developed a high-performance, coconut husk-based alternative that matches Styrofoam in durability and insulation. It is also competitively priced and environmentally friendly.

Another important challenge was dealing with the environmental harm caused by coconut husks, which are often burned or left to rot, leading to CO_2 emissions and waste. Fortuna transformed this agricultural byproduct into a resource by collecting husks from over 250 small-scale farms. They dried and pressed the husks into biodegradable insulation panels, each preventing approximately 7.5 kg of carbon emissions (Mekler, 2024; Cairns, 2021).

Scaling production brought additional logistical issues since processing large amounts of husks into consistent insulation required dependable systems. Fortuna tackled this by creating a decentralized supply chain and using hydraulic presses for efficient manufacturing of the liners (Manila Bulletin, 2024).

Finally, gaining market adoption was a challenge, particularly in persuading businesses to switch from familiar plastic foam to a new, natural fiber-based product. Strategic partnerships with companies like Grab Philippines helped validate their solution in the food delivery sector, while funding from ADB Ventures supported their scaling efforts and credibility (Mekler, 2023). Through this mix of innovation, sustainability, and strategic collaboration, Fortuna Cools has successfully navigated various obstacles to become a leader in eco-friendly packaging.

Figure 21 Journey of Fortuna Cools

Source: Created by Author by using Napkin.AI (https://www.napkin.ai/)

4.5 Algramo

> **"People are deciding between their pocket or their planet, so we need to be cheaper and better."** José Manuel Moller (UNEP, 2023)

Overview – José Manuel Moller started Algramo, which means "by the gram" in Spanish, in Chile in 2012. The company wanted to solve two big problems: the "poverty tax," which is the extra cost that low-income people have to pay when they have to buy things in little amounts, and the environmental damage caused by single-use plastic packaging. Algramo put smart, refillable dispensing equipment in neighborhood corner businesses to help solve these problems. Customers can buy things like rice, detergent, and cooking oil in reusable containers from these machines. Households can save 30–40 percent compared to supermarket costs by doing this, which makes it much easier for them to afford things (United Nations Environment Programme, 2023a). Moller said, "We're not just a platform for rich people who care about the environment; we're for people who just want to save money" (Michail, 2020). Algramo has put in more than 1,600 dispensers, reached hundreds of thousands of customers, allowed the reuse of more than 900,000 packing units, and stopped more than 100 tons of plastic trash since it started (United Nations Environment Programme, 2023b). Its unique business strategy has won it awards across the world, such as being named the most innovative firm in Latin America, winning the Ocean Plastic Innovation Challenge, and getting UNEP's 2023 Champion of the Earth Award for Entrepreneurial Vision (Michail, 2020). In short, Algramo combines social justice with environmental sustainability through a scalable, tech-driven paradigm. It lowers the cost of basic items and promotes a circular economy approach to daily use. Figure 22 provides a quick reference to the business overview of Algramo Company.

Need Addressed

Algramo deals with two problems that are linked. The first is the "poverty tax," which is the hidden cost that low-income families pay when they have to buy basic goods in little amounts at higher per-unit pricing. The second is the growing problem of plastic pollution caused by packaging that can only be used once. Algramo makes everyday items cheaper and easier to get by using clever dispensing devices and reusable containers.

Mission

Algramo's goal is to make sure that everyone can afford and get to important goods, no matter how much money they have. They also want to get rid of single-use plastics. The company gives customers the power to choose eco-friendly choices that fit with the ideas of a circular economy by using smart, reusable packaging methods. This helps the environment and society as a whole.

Where It All Began: The Journey of Algramo

The story of Algramo started with something that happened to the author. José Manuel Moller saw an unjust economic reality while studying at university and living in a poor area on the outskirts of Santiago, Chile. He and his neighbors

Algramo: The Circular Economy Model

Founded:2013
Leading Organisation: . Algramo
Headquarters: Santiago, Chile (with pilot expansions in NYC, Indonesia, and the UK)
Issue Addressed: The "poverty tax" on small-quantity purchases and plastic pollution from single-use packaging

Mission: Algramo aims to reduce both packaging waste and the poverty premium faced by low-income communities by delivering affordable, refillable product options through smart dispensing systems and reusable packaging. .

Technology : IoT-powered smart vending dispensers and RFID-enabled reusable containers connected via mobile app

Business Model: Both **B2B partnerships** with global brands (Unilever, Nestlé, Clorox, etc.) and **B2C channels** via a mobile app and community refill stations.

Value Proposition: Algramo offers **smart, reusable packaging and IoT-powered refill systems** that help eliminate single-use plastic and reduce the poverty premium for low-income consumer

Revenue Streams: Algramo earns revenue by partnering with global brands (like Unilever and Nestlé) to license its refill technology, selling smart reusable containers and refills through its app, and offering refill dispensers to retailers. It also generates income from data services and bulk orders for its dispensing systems.

SDGs Addressed: SDG1*, SDG9* ,SDG11*, SDG12*, SDG13*, SDG17*

Results

Environmental outcomes [From Inception till Year 2025]:
- ✓ Algramo's reuse system has prevented over 362 metric tons of carbon emissions;
- ✓ By reusing containers, the company has saved over 2.8 million liters of water;
- ✓ With 97.5 metric tons of plastic saved, Algramo is actively combating plastic pollution

Social outcomes [From Inception till Year 2025]:
- ✓ Over 325,000+ people accessed affordable essentials without overpaying
- ✓ Enabled 2,000+ local businesses (family stores) to offer bulk, cashless refills

Overview

Founded in Chile, Algramo created RFID-enabled reusable containers and IoT dispensing systems. These innovations let customers buy what they need, when they need it, without paying extra for packaging. This model removes the hidden cost of poverty while supporting zero-waste systems in both developed and emerging economies.

Key Stakeholders

Low-income consumers (benefit from affordable, bulk-priced essentials), Global CPG companies (Unilever, Nestlé, etc.), Retail store owners (host refill stations, generate revenue)Impact investors (Closed Loop Partners, MIT Solve, others), Municipal partners & NGOs

Challenges:

1. Initial consumer hesitation to switch from single-use packaging to refill systems due to unfamiliarity and habits
2. Managing the complexity of refill systems
3. Challenge related to single-use plastic packaging is cheap, widely available, and deeply ingrained in consumer habits

Key Success Factors:

1. Share the value propositions and explain the benefit of this new system for increasing the interest of consumers
2. Using the Combination of technology, logistics, and strategic partnerships for managing the complexity of refiill systems
3. By focusing on Affordable Pricing, Convenience, good strategic partnerships and incentives, company is focusing on solving the problem of competition

Source: **Algramo. (n.d.).** *Home page*. Retrieved August 13, 2025, from https://algramo.com/en/
SDG1: No Poverty ;SDG 9: Industry, Innovation, and Infrastructure; SDG 11: Sustainable Cities and Communities; SDG 12: Responsible Consumption and Production; SDG 13: Climate Action; SDG 17: Partnerships for the Goals

Figure 22 Profile of Algramo: Key Highlights

Source: Created by Author

had to pay extra for basic needs because they could only afford to buy tiny amounts from nearby corner businesses. The "poverty tax" was the difference in price. There was also the fact that every purchase came in single-use plastic packaging, which not only raised expenses but also made plastic pollution worse in neighborhoods that were already underserved.

Moller started Algramo in 2012 because he wanted to fight this unfairness. The name, which means "by the gram" in Spanish, reflects the main philosophy behind it: individuals should be able to buy exactly what they need at fair costs without being punished for not having enough money. Algramo worked with local stores and big name companies to offer things like rice, detergent, and cleaning supplies in containers that could be used again. A lot of these containers had smart chips in them, which let customers refill them at vending machines. This model not only made things cheaper, but it also cut down on plastic waste by a lot.

The business' effect grew as it got bigger. Algramo has kept more than 100 tons of plastic trash out of landfills and allowed more than 900,000 packing units to be reused by 2020. This shows that social fairness and sustainability can work together. Moller's leadership got more attention around the world because of this success. In 2023, he was named Vice Chair of the UN Advisory Board of Eminent Persons on Zero Waste. This confirmed his position as a global leader in the circular economy. The United Nations Environment Programme (UNEP) gave him its highest environmental award, the Champions of the Earth, in the category of Entrepreneurial Vision in that same year. This award recognized not only Algramo's creative ideas for packaging and pricing, but also its larger goal of making sustainability available and cheap for everyone.

Figure 23 shows Algramo's voyage in a picture.

Challenges and Success Factors

"The challenge around sustainability is not only about technology, it is also about consumer behaviour. I started thinking about how I could make people fall in love with an empty bottle," Moller said. (UNEP, 2023a)

Algramo faced several major challenges during its journey. It needed to change consumer habits, manage logistical issues, and secure partnerships with large companies. At first, it was hard to convince consumers to move from traditional single-use packaging to reusable refill systems. People were used to their buying habits and were skeptical about new technologies.

Setting up a wide network of smart dispensing machines in low-income neighborhoods also presented logistical hurdles. These included distribution,

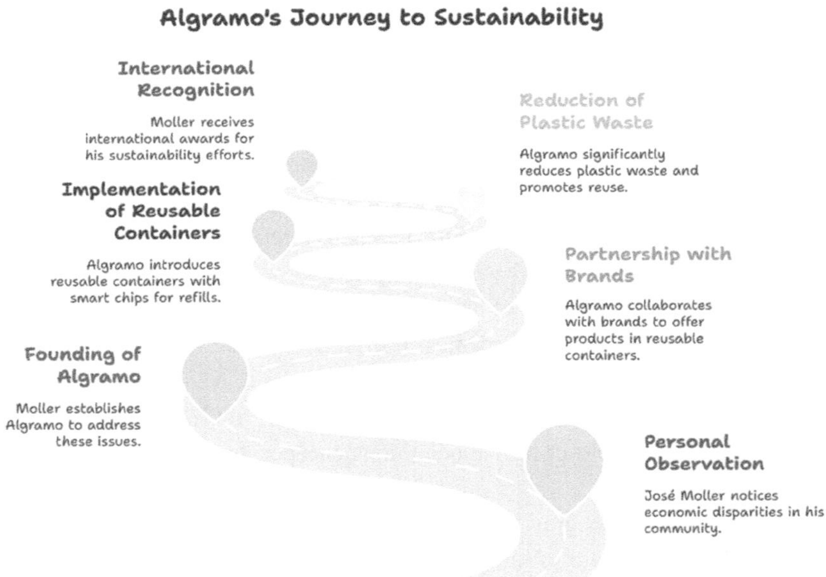

Figure 23 Journey of Algramo

Source: Created by Author by using Napkin.AI (https://www.napkin.ai/)

maintenance, and access for customers. Another challenge was earning the trust of major consumer goods companies so they would adopt Algramo's innovative refillable packaging model.

To address these challenges, Algramo focused on engaging with the community and educating people about the environmental and economic benefits of refillable packaging. They created user-friendly smart dispensers and included mobile payment systems to make the refill process easier. This improved accessibility and convenience.

Algramo believes that the solution to plastic pollution must not only be for high-income millennial vegetarians," said Moller. "This should be designed for everyone, who, at the end of the day, make decisions based on price. So, the approach of Algramo has always been affordability." (UNEP, 2023a)

The company also formed strong partnerships with industry leaders like Unilever. This collaboration helped them scale their model and confirm their approach. Through ongoing innovation and strategic partnerships, Algramo effectively tackled behavioral, operational, and corporate obstacles. This allowed them to establish themselves as a leading sustainable solution in Latin America's retail sector.

In the last we are sharing what the Founder has an overview about the company

By creating low-cost reusable packaging and reducing the cost of distribution through our vending machines and dispenser system, we dramatically cut costs for customers and allow them to purchase small quantities of products at an affordable price. This benefits brands too who want to sell product, not packaging. Our system easily integrates into local bodegas, large grocery store chains, and can be delivered to a customer's home through our mobile delivery app. Cote, Founder and CEO of Algramo, (Closed loop Partners, 2020a)

4.6 Ecocitex

> **Ecocitex is an opportunity. It's a project where together we can reduce textile waste and create great social impact that you can communicate. We are all working toward a shared goal: to eliminate textile waste. (NESst)**
>
> — Rosario Hevia

Overview

Ecocitex is a mission-driven company based in Santiago, Chile. It focuses on addressing the growing textile waste crisis in the country, primarily caused by the fast fashion industry. Each year, about 39,000 tons of clothing are thrown away, especially in Chile's desert areas (NESsT, n.d.). Ecocitex aims to change this situation. The company was founded by entrepreneur Rosario Hevia. Its main goal is to eliminate textile waste by giving old clothes a new life. Three years ago, Ecocitex opened a recycling facility in Santiago that processes around 69 tons of donated and used clothing every year. However, its impact extends beyond just reducing waste.

Ecocitex also runs a clothing donation program that helps underserved communities. Since 2022, it has distributed over 1.2 tons of clothing, directly improving the lives of about 220 people each year (NESsT, n.d.). The production facility does more than recycle clothing; it also creates job opportunities. The company hires and trains women who were previously incarcerated, enabling them to enter skilled technical roles that are often male-dominated. This commitment to inclusion is a key part of Ecocitex's approach. In addition to selling upcycled and second-hand products through local stores, Ecocitex collaborates with community-based sewing professionals. Most of these individuals are women and come from marginalized backgrounds. They repurpose materials into new products. Currently, more than 80 percent of their production partners are women, and 35 percent are from excluded or vulnerable groups. By supporting these artisans and small workshops, Ecocitex is reducing waste while also building local skills, livelihoods, and economic strength. Figure 24 provides a quick reference to the business overview of Ecocitex Company.

Ecocitex: The Circular Economy Model

Founded: 2020
Leading Organisation: Ecocitex
Headquarters: Santiago, Chile
Issue Addressed: Addresses textile waste and social exclusion by recycling discarded clothes into yarn without water or chemicals

Mission: Eliminate Textile waste generated by Fashion Industry and promote Circular Economy

Technology : Dry mechanical recycling process

Business Model: Circular economy model mainly **B2C** recycled yarns, clothing, and sustainable products through its **own store and website**.

Value Proposition: Recycled yarn, upcycled clothing, Eco Friendly Accessories, Donation Kits.

Revenue Streams: Sale of Recycled Products, Clothing Donation & Recycled Kits

SDGs Addressed: SDG5*, SDG8*, SDG10*, SDG12*, SDG13*, SDG15*

Results

Environmental outcomes [From Inception till Year 2025]:
- ✓ Recycled 209 tons of clothing, equivalent to 136,000 reused garments and 4,380 donated, preventing the emission of 1,200 tons of CO2
- ✓ 1,357 tons of CO_2 emissions mitigated (based on USACH Study); 269,000 garments reused

Social outcomes [From Inception till Year 2025]:
- ✓ 8,145 garments donated;
- ✓ 18 people involved in reintegration through employment or training;
- ✓ Employs women prisoners and people in social reintegration for part of the process

Overview

Ecocitex was founded in 2020 with a mission to tackle Chile's growing textile waste crisis. The company focuses on two main solutions: reselling second-hand clothes that are still in good condition and upcycling discarded textiles into new materials like recycled yarn and sustainable products. Beyond environmental impact, Ecocitex is also committed to social inclusion, especially by providing employment opportunities for women, including those from marginalized communities.

Key Stakeholders

Donors (Public/Consumers), Customers(B2B and B2C), Employees (especially women), Partner orgnaizations, Government and Policy Makers.

Challenges:

1) Challenge to dispose the clothes which cannot be upcycled or upsold.
2) Sorting garments, managing waste clothing, and launching upcycling at scale.
3) Many people don't distinguish between donation (for good clothes) and recycling (for unusable items), creating confusion and contamination in the supply chain.
4) Operating losses during first three years, with more clothing received than sold.
5) A devastating fire destroyed the factory, machines, inventory, and the store.

Key Success Factors:

1) Identified a major challenge in disposing of clothes that cannot be upcycled or resold — a gap that led her to launch **Ecocitex** to address this pressing issue.
2) Developed a clear sorting process: sell/donate good items, upcycle worn ones into accessories, and recycle rest.
3) Ecocitex introduced participation fees to emphasize that drop-offs of bad quality clothing are part of a service and needs engagement—reinforcing the educational aspect.
4) Introduce Ecocitex Club- Memebership model for resolving the financial crunch
5) Partnered with NESsT to rebuild operations, redesign financial and logistic models, and stay true to circular model

Source: Ecocitex. (n.d.). *Misión, historia y equipo* [Mission, history, and team]. Retrieved June 14, 2025, from https://www.ecocitex.cl/pages/mision-historia-y-equipo-ecocitex
SDG 5:Gender Equality; SDG 8:Decent Work and Economic Growth; SDG 10: Reduce Inequalities; SDG 12: Responsible Consumption and Production; SDG 13: Climate Action,; SDG 15: Life on Land.

Figure 24 Profile of Ecocitex: Key Highlights

Source: Created by Author

Need Addressed

Chile faces a growing textile waste crisis, with over 39,000 tons discarded annually, much of it ending up in landfills. There is also a lack of inclusive job opportunities for women, especially those from marginalized backgrounds

Mission Statement

Ecocitex is dedicated to eliminating textile waste by transforming discarded clothing into high-quality yarn using circular economy technologies. It is committed to empowering women and marginalized communities by providing meaningful employment and technical training, fostering sustainable livelihoods while promoting environmental responsibility.

Where It All Began: The Journey of Ecocitex

Ecocitex started when its founder, Rosario Hevia, saw the problem of textile waste. She saw perfectly nice kids' clothes being thrown away only because they had gender labels on them while she was in the clinic with her newborn son in 2018. The first girl child onesies she bought didn't fit her baby boy. This trash inspired her, and with her skills in engineering, she created Travieso, a second-hand baby clothes market in Santiago. But this project caused another problem: more and more unusable, worn-out garments were being thrown away. By the end of 2019, Hevia was acquiring 400 kg of textiles that were causing problems every month. She looked for ways to recycle and contacted environmental groups and big stores. Sadly, she got ambiguous answers like "we donate it," She kept saying, "But I'm talking about the clothes that are in bad shape, and they said, 'Oh, no, they're thrown away.'" At the moment, she couldn't discover any good solutions in Chile (Miliani, 2022).

Hevia bought a closed yarn plant at the end of 2019 because he wanted to make a difference. This was a turning moment, a way to deal with a problem that was happening all over the place. Ecocitex was founded with that facility. Its name is short for Economía Circular Textil, which means "Textile Circular Economy."

She thought the factory could manage up to 20 tons of textile waste every month. This was a big objective for a country that sends about 550 tons of trash to landfills every year. Images of a 39,000-ton clothes graveyard in Chile's Atacama Desert that went viral in 2021 made this expedition even more important (Rembre, 2024). Hevia didn't feel overwhelmed; instead, she became more motivated. "The problem got a lot of attention around the world, but not the solution," she said.

In Santiago, Ecocitex has a tiny recycling station in its courtyard where visitors may drop off items for a modest fee. The clothes must be free of buttons and zippers. This charge isn't a punishment; it has two objectives. It helps pay for labor and shows the difference between recycling and giving away.

You donate clothes in good condition, it's like donating a washing machine that still works, but when something is broken or stained, that's a recycling service.," Hevia explains (Miliani, 2022).

Clothes are carefully sorted within the factory. Things are sorted into groups so they can be sold again, turned into accessories, or shredded by color to make bright yarn without needing water or dyes. The facility runs almost without waste and processes roughly one ton of textiles every week, which is just enough to meet current demand.

A burgeoning network of micro-entrepreneurs is helping Ecocitex's yarn reach customers in stores and online. There are already 67 shops and designers in Chile who are supporting a new wave of environmentally friendly design. Hevia stays hopeful during this process. Within two years, the brand gathered over 160,000 social media followers and received a lot of media coverage (Miliani, 2022). "We're finally talking about the issue." The next step is action." In addition to the textual analysis, we provide a visual representation of the company's journey in Figure 25.

Navigating the Path to Sustainability

Ecocitex has had its share of problems along the way, especially in its early years. One of the hardest things was dealing with clothes that couldn't be reused or sold again. The original plan was to sort and recycle textile waste, but the

Figure 25 Journey of Ecocitex

Source: Created by Author by using Napkin.AI (https://www.napkin.ai/)

crew immediately saw that most of the clothes that were given were in such bad shape that they couldn't be sold or used again. A lot of donors had a hard time telling the difference between giving away clothes that were in good condition and just getting rid of textiles that weren't useful. This mix-up in the supply chain caused contamination, wasted time, and made the sorting procedure much more difficult.

Adding more operations simply made things worse. It took a lot of work, space, and well-organized systems to sort, manage, and upcycle at a large scale. This was hard for Ecocitex's tiny workforce and limited resources. The first few years were extremely hard on the wallet. Even though the group got a lot of gifts, it couldn't process or sell items fast enough to be in business. It lost money for the first three years. Things got worse when a terrible fire destroyed the plant, taking with it important machines, goods, and even their store. This could have been the end for a tiny business. It turned out to be a turning point instead. Ecocitex worked with NESsT, a group that helps social enterprises, to reorganize their operations, redesign their financial models, and improve their logistics – all while staying true to their goal of a circular economy.

Ecocitex also improved how it sorts things at the same time. There were three types of clothes: clothes that could be sold or given away, clothes that could be turned into accessories, and clothes that were too worn out to be used again and could be made into yarn. The organization added a participation charge to make things clearer for donors and make sure they were responsible. This price made it obvious that sending off clothes that couldn't be used was more than just a donation; it was a recycling operation that needed money and time to handle.

Ecocitex started the "Ecocitex Club," a subscription-based membership concept, to improve its finances and get more people involved in the community. This program not only helped keep revenue steady, but it also gave members a chance to learn about sustainable fashion and get more involved in the cause.

Ecocitex turned its problems into opportunities by being strong, flexible, and working with others. Every problem, whether it was operational, financial, or structural, was a chance to make the organization stronger and more effective at achieving its objective.

4.7 Africa Collect Textiles

> **"Discussions abroad were beginning to center around creating circular economies, but I knew that global trade could never become circular unless we protected the recipients of the waste," explained Stroomer.** (Ndambuki, 2024)

Overview

Africa Collect Textiles Ltd (ACT) is a social enterprise based in Nairobi. It was founded in 2014 by Elmar Stroomer and Alex Musembi. The company tackles the environmental and social issues related to textile waste in Kenya. ACT collects, sorts, and upcycles used garments. They install clothing collection bins in busy areas like malls and universities to encourage donations of clean, unwanted clothes. Wearable items are sold at affordable prices through local women's groups. Non-wearable textiles are turned into new products, such as rugs, bags, and baskets. This process creates a local circular economy and supports sustainable development. Figure 26 provides a quick reference to the business overview of African Collect Textiles.

Need Addressed

According to EEA data, around 46 percent of textiles discarded by European countries end up in Africa, and 41 percent in Asia (Lecumberri, 2024). In Africa, while there is demand for cheap second-hand clothing from Europe, Greenpeace reports that 40 percent of these clothes are not sold and end up being burned or dumped in landfills (Lecumberri, 2024). Recognizing this alarming issue, the founders of Africa Collect Textiles established the company to tackle textile waste through reuse, recycling, and upcycling – turning discarded clothing into new, useful products.

Mission Statement

African Collect Textile focus on environmental conservation by enabling a circular economy for textiles and footwear. It utilizes resources to their full potential, supports communities that are affected by textile waste and generates new jobs in collecting, sorting and upcycling of used textiles.

Where It All Began: The Journey of Africa Collect Textiles

Africa Collect Textiles Ltd (ACT) began when co-founders Elmar Stroomer and Alex Musembi observed a problem while working in the Netherlands. They collected used clothing for resale as second-hand items in countries like Kenya. They saw a noticeable gap; the Netherlands had over 10,000 drop-off points for used garments, while Kenya, with a population three times larger, had fewer than 100.

"The Netherlands had more than 10,000 collection points for people to drop off their used garments, but Kenya had less than 100," Stroomer explained in an interview with Powering SMEs. (Ndambuki, 2024)

Africa Collect Textiles: The Circular Economy Model

Founded: 2014
Leading Organisation: Africa Collect Textiles Ltd
Headquarters: Nairobi, Kenya
Issue Addressed: Addresses the dual challenge of textile waste and social exclusion by upcycling discarded clothing and creating employment opportunities for women

Mission: Close the global fashion loop" by breaking the vicious cycle of a linear fashion system.

Technology : Manual Collection and Sorting & Handcrafted Upcycling Techniques

Business Model: Circular economy model **: B2C** - Collections from consumers; selling upcycled goods (decor items, accessories) **B2B** Supplying recycled materials and collaborating with businesses for co-creation

Value Proposition:: Recycling and upcycling discarded clothing into eco-friendly accessories such as backpacks, rugs, baskets, and toys—promoting circular fashion while reducing textile waste.

Revenue Streams: Sale of Recycled and upcycled Products, Clothing Donation,

SDGs Addressed: SDG5*, SDG8*, SDG10* , SDG12*, SDG13*, SDG15*

Results

Environmental outcomes [From Inception till Year 2025]:
- ✓ 171 kg of textiles diverted from landfill;
- ✓ 1,379,641 kg of carbon dioxide mitigated.

Social outcomes [From Inception till Year 2025]:
- ✓ As of July 2025; 200 jobs created (direct + indirect employment) especially for women

Overview

Africa Collect Textiles is driving the circularity of fashion in Africa. Through innovative upcycling and recycling they turn textile waste into value, blending Africa's rich craftsmanship with infrastructure that empowers communities for a sustainable future. Focus on environmental conservation by enabling a circular economy for textiles and footwear.

Key Stakeholders

Donors (Public/Consumers), Customers(B2B and B2C), Employees (especially women), Partner orgnaizations, Government and Policy Makers.

Challenges:

1. Difficulty arranging funds to set up and expand the organization.
2. Inadequate infrastructure for large-scale collection, sorting, and recycling of textile waste
3. .Overcoming customer expectations of low prices despite using free raw materials.
4. Competition from local and cheaper brands for upcycled products
5. .Low consumer awareness about the benefits of recycled textiles.
6. Insufficient current infrastructure to meet growing demand and scale operations.

Key Success Factors:

1. Secured investment and partnerships, including funding from impact investors like Shein, to support growth.
2. Developed localized collection hubs and invested in scalable sorting technology to improve efficiency.
3. Focused on educating customers about the value and quality of upcycled products to justify pricing.
4. Differentiated products through quality, design, and storytelling to build a loyal customer base.
5. Launched awareness campaigns and collaborations with fashion influencers to promote sustainable textiles.
6. Gradually expanded infrastructure and operational capacity aligned with market demand and funding.

Source: Africa Collect Textiles. (n.d.). *Home*. https://africacollecttextiles.com/
SDG 5:Gender Equality; SDG 8:Decent Work and Economic Growth; SDG 10: Reduce Inequalities; SDG 12: Responsible Consumption and Production; SDG 13: Climate Action,; SDG 15: Life on Land.

Figure 26 Profile of Africa collect textiles: Key Highlights

Source: Created by Author

Driven by the need for change, Elmar and Alex launched ACT in 2014 as a side project with a clear mission: to upcycle used clothing and create a circular textile ecosystem in Africa. Their vision was strong, but the journey was challenging.

"At first, we struggled to find funding because many investors thought our idea was strange. They didn't see the value in collecting textile waste in a country with so many second-hand clothes," Stroomer shared. (Ndambuki, 2024)

Despite initial doubts, their determination paid off in 2020 when ACT secured its first funding during the peak of the COVID-19 pandemic. This marked a crucial turning point. With new support, the team expanded their collection network and invested in machinery.

Today, they have established forty-two collection points in busy areas, encouraging the public to donate unwanted, clean, and dry clothes. The donated clothing takes one of two paths. If it is wearable, it is bundled into mitumba bales and sold at lower-than-market prices to women's groups in local second-hand markets. If it is unwearable, ACT upcycles the garments at their facility in Baba Dogo, Nairobi, turning them into products like backpacks, rugs, baskets, and toys. These items are sold in local and international markets, including the Netherlands, UK, and Germany.

ACT also sources raw materials from offcuts of clothing industries, unsellable second-hand items from markets like Gikomba, and even uniforms from security firms.

Even with a solid business model, raising awareness remains a challenge. ACT currently processes about 3,000 to 4,000 kilograms of textile waste each month but has much bigger goals. With help from partners like the Kenya Climate Innovation Center, they aim to scale up to over a million kilograms over the next three years. This expansion will help reduce product costs and lessen their reliance on grants.

ACT is also pushing for policy changes. They argue that Extended Producer Responsibility (EPR) fees – taxes brands pay to manage end-of-life waste should benefit the African countries that actually handle the disposal. In addition to the textual analysis, we provide a visual representation of the company's journey in Figure 27.

Navigating the Path to Sustainability

Africa Collect Textiles Ltd (ACT) has faced significant but clear challenges on its journey to building a sustainable textile recycling model in Kenya. One of the earliest and most pressing issues was securing funding.

As co-founder Willemijn Stroomer explained, *"At first, we had challenges in raising funding because a lot of investors thought we were odd. They didn't see*

Figure 27 Journey of Africa Collect Textiles

Source: Created by Author by using Napkin.AI (https://www.napkin.ai/)

the economic value in collecting textile waste in a country that had so many second hand clothes."

This skepticism made it hard for ACT to get the capital needed to build proper infrastructure for collecting, sorting, and recycling used textiles.

ACT also struggled with public perception regarding product pricing. Stroomer pointed out that *"Pricing has been an issue for us because people believe that since our raw materials are free, our products should be cheap. At the moment, that isn't the case, but if we can grow our capacity, then our products will become more mainstream."* (Ndambuki, 2024)

This misunderstanding about the cost of upcycling has been a barrier, but the team believes that as they scale, the value of their work will become more visible and better accepted.

The company is also working hard to raise awareness about textile waste and its environmental impact.

Communication manager Nathalie Naina highlighted the seriousness of the issue, saying, *"When these clothes reach the landfills, they are either burnt to reduce their volume or they are left to decay. What we do not know is that some of the clothes that are being made right now take almost 200 years to decompose."* (Ndambuki, 2024)

To address this, ACT is not only recycling but also educating consumers. They are helping people see their products differently. As Stroomer shared, *"We are able to tell people that this is not just a basket or a carpet but is actually made from jeans material, it immediately invokes a sense of a more conscious buying decision."*

Moreover, ACT emphasizes responsible donation practices. *It doesn't matter whether they are wearable or not, all we ask is for people to donate their clothes clean and dry, if they are wet, oily or stained that becomes waste and it has to be discarded,* Stroomer clarified. Their model even challenges the perception of second-hand clothing, with Stroomer remarking, *In a sense, we are taking back the mtumba to where it came from, but now we are selling it in better shape than it was when it came.* (Ndambuki, 2024)

Through a combination of environmental education, transparent storytelling, and commitment to quality, ACT is turning its challenges into opportunities and laying the foundation for a more circular and sustainable textile economy in Africa.

4.8 Salubata

> **Thus far, we have sold over 6,000 pairs of shoes, and these shoes are made from recycled plastic waste and our net offset is about 145.9 kilograms of CO_2 per shoe, said Salubata co-founder Yewande Adebowale.** (Musmanni, 2023)

Overview

Salubata was founded in 2020 by Fela Buyi Akinse and Yewande Akinse. The company aims to cut down plastic waste in landfills and waterways by turning it into raw material for their innovative, modular shoes, which is the main product. This process reduces waste and meets the growing demand for affordable, sustainable footwear. According to Yewande Akinse, the company has sold over 6,000 pairs of shoes and has converted 150,000 pieces of plastic waste into shoes. This effort has directly helped reduce the carbon footprint (Guardian Nigeria, 2024).

In a a statement by the founder and CEO, Fela Buyi he stated that

Salubata's philosophy is the belief that footwear should not only enhance an outfit but also provide unparalleled comfort. The brand understands that

modern consumers lead dynamic lives, often transitioning from professional settings to casual outings, and thus require versatile footwear that can keep up with their pace. Salubata's collection features a wide array of designs, from chic heels to stylish sneakers, all meticulously crafted to ensure that every step is taken with confidence and ease. The use of high-quality materials ensures durability, while innovative sole technology provides cushioning and support, making Salubata shoes a perfect choice for all-day wear. (Ajiboye, 2025)

Sustainability is an important value at Salubata. It shows a trend in the fashion industry toward eco-friendly practices. The brand is dedicated to reducing its environmental impact by using sustainable materials and ethical production methods. This commitment appeals to consumers who are more aware of how their choices affect the planet. Salubata's efforts help create a healthier environment and set an example for other brands, demonstrating that style and sustainability can work well together. Figure 28 provides a quick reference to the business overview of Salubata Company.

Need Addressed

> *The drainages are choked with plastic bottles and with waste. So whenever it rains, Lagos is always flooded. We started imagining how we could solve this problem – and the plastic plague is not just limited to Lagos; it is a global problem. So we started imagining how we could use our lifestyles to solve the global plastic plague,* said Yewande. (Musmanni, 2023)

Salubata addresses several important environmental issues with its innovative footwear solutions. The company tackles Nigeria's huge plastic pollution problem, where over 5.8 million tons of plastic waste are generated each year, by recycling plastic into modular shoes (Fremong, 2022). This helps reduce waste and fights against the low global plastic recycling rate. Traditional shoe production uses a lot of resources and produces significant carbon emissions. However, Salubata's modular design lets users replace only parts of the shoe, which lowers both waste and emissions. Each pair of shoes is carbon-offset, and the company is also developing technology to convert CO_2 into oxygen, further reducing its environmental impact. With this approach, Salubata combines sustainability, design, and innovation to promote a circular economy and a cleaner planet.

Mission Statement

Salubata's mission is to create innovative lifestyle technologies that benefit both people and the planet. The company focuses on turning plastic waste into sustainable, modular footwear. This approach tackles environmental pollution

Salubata: The Circular Economy Model

Founded: 2020
Leading Organisation: Salubata
Headquarters: Nigeria, France, United States
Issue Addressed: Tackles the problem of plastic pollution by creating sustainable shoes from recycled waste.

Mission: To transform plastic waste into innovative, sustainable footwear that empowers communities, reduces environmental pollution, and promotes a circular economy through creativity and social impact.

Technology : Modular shoe design technology combined with recycled plastic processing techniques

Business Model: Circular economy model mainly focusing on B2C (selling sustainable, customizable shoes directly to eco-conscious consumers) and also engaged in B2B at some level.

Value Proposition: Salubata's value proposition lies in offering stylish, customizable footwear made from recycled plastic waste, providing eco-conscious consumers with sustainable, affordable, and durable shoes that help reduce environmental pollution while promoting circular fashion.

Revenue Streams: Direct sales of modular, sustainable shoes to consumers (online and offline)Partnerships and collaborations with retailers or platforms (e.g., Amazon)Grants and investment funding from organizations like NBA and Techstars (for growth and scaling)Possibly custom orders or corporate bulk sales (B2B)

SDGs Addressed: SDG6*,,SDG7*, SDG9*, SDG11*, SDG12*

Results

Environmental outcomes [From Inception till Dec 2024]:

- ✓ Converted 150,000 plastic wastes to shoes;
- ✓ Approximately 145.9 kg CO_2 emissions avoided for each pair of modular shoes sold

Social outcomes [From Inception till Dec 2024]:

- ✓ Collaborates with ~50 waste collectors, many of whom are women,
- ✓ Providing income for underserved communities

Overview

Salubata is a Nigerian footwear company that creates modular shoes made from recycled plastic waste. Founded by Fela Buyi Akinse and Yewande Akinse, the company focuses on sustainable fashion while addressing environmental pollution. Salubata also supports social impact by allocating a portion of its profits to empower underserved communities, combining innovation with purpose.

Key Stakeholders

Investors (NBA, Techstars), Partners (Amazon, Techstars Accelerator), Employees and Team Members, Customers and End Users (Eco-conscious consumers worldwide), Community and Social Impact(Underserved children and women).

Challenges:

1. Transitioning from Leather to Recycled Materials
2. Confronted difficulty in attracting Investors and forming partnerships
3. Challenge to create a customizable, modular shoe from recycled plastic
4. Transforming plastic waste into high-quality, wearable shoes that meet international standards was a huge hurdle
5. Challenge to Build a Skilled Team and Community Engagement.

Key Success Factors:

1. Innovated a process to upcycle plastic waste into wearable, durable footwear
2. Salubata entered and won global competitions (e.g., Hack the Normal and New European Bauhaus Prize) and was selected for prestigious accelerator programs like **Techstars Los Angeles**.
3. Invested heavily in R&D to develop a patented modular design that allows consumers to change shoe parts (like uppers and soles) without replacing the entire product
4. Committed 5% of its profits to empower women and children in underserved communities. They implemented training programs to upskill locals, especially women, and engaged them in their value chain

Source: Salubata. (n.d.). *Salubata – Official website*. Retrieved August 15, 2025, from https://www.salubataofficial.com
SDG 6: Clean Water and Sanitation, SDG 7: Affordable and Clean Energy, SDG 9: Industry, Innovation and Infrastructure, SDG 11: Sustainable Cities and Communities, SDG 12: Responsible Consumption and Production

Figure 28 Profile of Salubata: Key Highlights

Source: Created by Author

and promotes a circular economy. Through its patented technologies, including shoes that decompose carbon, Salubata aims to reduce carbon emissions and lessen the fashion industry's ecological impact. The company also cares about social impact. It empowers underprivileged communities, especially women and children, by donating a portion of its profits to their development. Overall, Salubata wants to bring together sustainability, innovation, and social responsibility to create practical solutions for environmental and social issues.

Where It All Began: The Journey of Salubata

Prior to starting Salubata, co-founder Fela Buyi worked in various roles, including shoe designer and business analyst for a leather shoe brand in Lagos, Nigeria. There, he learned about shoe designs and gained detailed knowledge about the shoe manufacturing process. Before this, he was an environmental scientist, focusing on pollution. In that role, he observed large amounts of plastic waste throughout the city and in sewage systems. This experience with plastic waste pollution sparked his brainstorming. He began to think of a new solution to reduce the plastic waste in the environment (Fremong, 2022).

"I thought, if I could reduce the volume of plastic by crushing the bottle itself, maybe we could provide a potential solution to this problem of plastic pollution," Buyi said. (Musmanni, 2023)

Buyi consistently takes the road less travelled. For example, when he was in college, he opted for a more difficult computer science program, just for the sake of being different.

I ended up cramming and forgot what I had learned before the exam and it didn't end up working. If I had prepared well it could have worked. That's why I say entrepreneurship is not about going a different route necessarily but instead having the right tools to solve a problem. (Musmanni, 2023)

When it was time to find solutions for plastic waste pollution, Buyi's innovative thinking, along with his background in science and shoe design, helped him create a strong solution. Salubata's main mission focuses on addressing plastic waste, which is a significant environmental issue in Nigeria and around the world (Fremong, 2022). The company uses recycled plastic collected from waterways and landfills to make its shoes. This process not only cuts down on waste but also meets the urgent need for affordable, sustainable footwear options. According to Yewande Akinse, the company has sold over 6,000 pairs of shoes and has converted 150,000 pieces of plastic waste into shoes, helping to reduce the carbon footprint. Each pair of shoes sold offsets about 145.9 kilograms of CO_2, showing the real impact of their efforts (Guardian Nigeria, 2024).

Figure 29 Journey of Salubata

Source: Created by Author by using Napkin.AI (https://www.napkin.ai/)

The company's operations are important for dealing with climate issues in Nigeria, which has experienced severe flooding because of climate change. By tackling plastic waste, Salubata helps reduce drainage problems that lead to flooding. This situation has impacted millions and caused significant loss of life. The company's initiative promotes environmental sustainability and also addresses public health issues related to stagnant water and waste buildup. In addition to the textual analysis, we provide a visual representation of the company's journey in Figure 29.

Navigating Path to Sustainability

Salubata, a Nigerian footwear company focusing on cleantech, faced several major challenges as it started to build a sustainable and impactful brand. Initially, the founders focused on producing leather shoes but soon saw the environmental damage caused by leather. Co-founder Fela Akinse, who is an environmental scientist, led a crucial change by creating a process to turn plastic waste into wearable, modular footwear. This marked an important shift from traditional materials to sustainable options (Guardian.ng).

Another significant challenge was developing a customizable, modular shoe made from recycled plastic. This required extensive research and testing to make sure the shoes were not only eco-friendly but also functional, durable, and appealing to consumers. The result was a patented design featuring interchangeable uppers connected to algae-based foam soles with zippers. This allowed customers to customize their shoes without having to buy multiple pairs. As Akinse explained, *Instead of you buying extra shoes, you can just have [several different] top flaps ... so you have a full wardrobe of shoes that uses less material* (Spectrum IEEE).

Turning plastic waste into high-quality, breathable footwear also came with its own set of challenges. To solve this, Salubata improved its production process, making shoes that are 75 percent cheaper than traditional models, yet stylish and comfortable enough for international markets.

Akinse pointed out, *They are also affordable because they cost at least 75 percent less than what our competitors offer* (Climate-KIC). In addition to production, attracting investors and forming strategic partnerships posed another challenge. To gain global recognition, Salubata took part in and won global competitions like the New European Bauhaus Prize and got into programs such as Techstars Los Angeles. These opportunities increased their visibility and led to collaborations with major partners like Amazon and NBA Africa (PM News Nigeria, Wikipedia).

Finally, forming a team that shared Salubata's commitment to sustainability and community inclusion was essential. The company dedicated 5 percent of its profits to empower women and children in underserved areas through training programs and jobs within their production chain. As stated in their New European Bauhaus application, these funds are used to "train them in the art of footwear design and manufacturing and employ them as our staff."

Akinse emphasized the team's importance by saying, *Our team of highly intelligent people – with great skill sets necessary for scale has provided us with great inputs to grow* (ATQ News). Through innovation, resilience, and purpose, Salubata overcame these foundational challenges and is emerging as a significant player in sustainable fashion and circular economy innovation.

4.9 Gjenge Makers

> **Plastic waste is everywhere and it's not going anywhere. The question is what we do with it. What you see as waste, I see as the foundation for something greater, said Matee. (RFI, 2025)**

Overview

Gjenge Makers is a Kenyan social enterprise founded in 2017 by Nzambi Matee, a mechanical engineer and environmentalist. The aim is to turn plastic waste into durable and eco-friendly construction bricks. The company is based in Nairobi, a city that produces about 500 to 550 tons of plastic waste every day (Houser, 2021). It started in response to the serious plastic pollution seen in the streets and landfills of urban Kenya.

Worldwide, more than 380 million tons of plastic are produced each year, but less than 10 percent gets recycled properly. A lot of it ends up in landfills and oceans, which poses major environmental and public health risks. To tackle this issue, Matee developed a custom low-tech machine that shreds, melts, and compresses plastic waste mixed with sand. This process creates bricks that are up to seven times stronger than concrete while being lighter and cheaper. Figure 30 provides a quick reference to the business overview of Gjenge Makers.

Need Addressed

Gjenge Makers addresses the problem of large amounts of plastic waste in Kenya by transforming it into strong, affordable, and practical construction products, such as various types of bricks. This approach not only provides sustainable building materials but also contributes to the circular economy.

Mission Statement: To transform plastic waste into durable, affordable construction materials that promote environmental sustainability and advance the circular economy, while empowering local communities in Kenya through innovative and socially responsible manufacturing.

Where It All Began: The Journey of Gjenge Makers

Gjenge Makers started in 2017 when Kenyan materials engineer and physicist Nzambi Matee left her job in the oil industry to address rising plastic pollution in Nairobi. She worked from a small backyard lab at her mother's home and spent months perfecting a mix of plastic and sand. This effort led to the first functional brick prototype by 2018. In 2019, Matee built her own hydraulic press, using machinery from a scrapyard, to increase the production of plastic-sand bricks made from shredded, unsorted plastic waste and sand.

Her innovation quickly gained traction. By 2020, with seed funding and guidance from the UNEP Young Champions of the Earth award, Gjenge Makers began full-scale operations to produce durable, eco-friendly bricks and paving blocks. Production increased to 1,000 to 1,500 bricks a day, recycling about 500 kilograms of plastic daily.

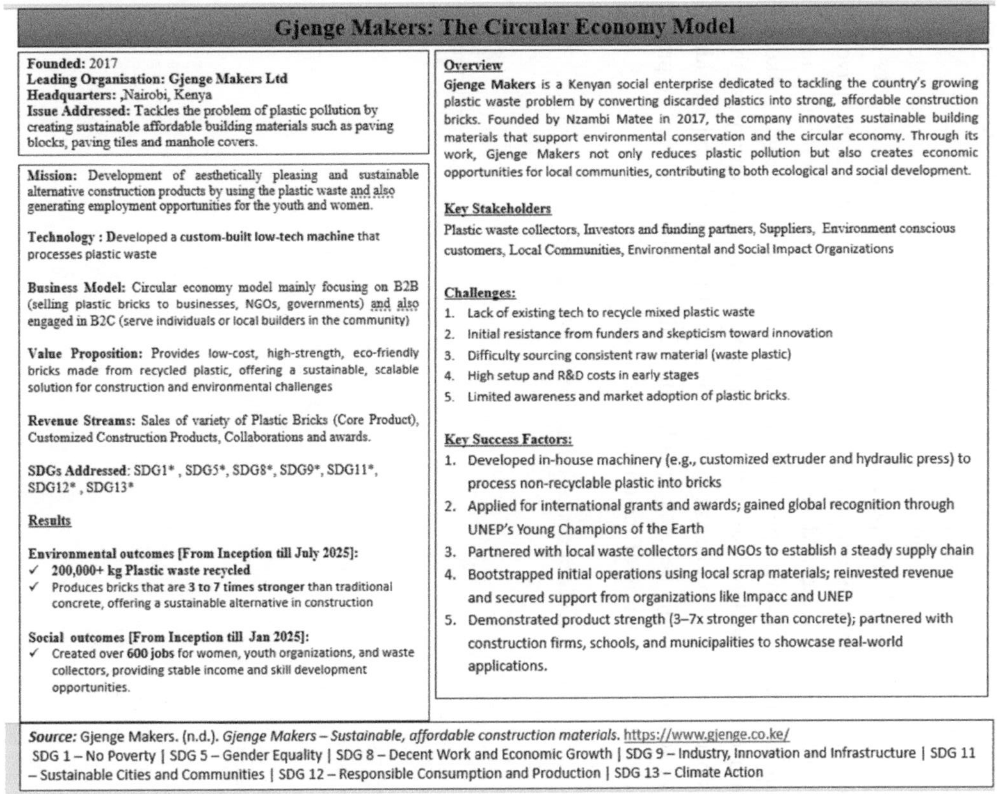

Figure 30 Profile of Gjenge Makers: Key Highlights

Source: Created by Author

By March 2021, the company had turned twenty metric tons of previously unusable plastic into building materials. Their bricks were three to seven times stronger than concrete, lighter, cost-effective, and well-suited to local climate needs. These bricks were soon used for paving roads, sidewalks, school areas, and gardens across Nairobi. Community integration has been essential from the beginning. Gjenge Makers employed around 112 local people, focusing on women and youth from low-income backgrounds. This provided stable jobs, training, and economic empowerment.

As the business grew, it attracted international attention for its practical circular economy model and potential for sustainable infrastructure. As of 2023 to 2024, the company continued to expand, producing up to 3,000 pavers daily, while demand exceeded capacity. This reflects both community and commercial interest in their products. In just a few years, Gjenge Makers transformed from a backyard experiment into a scalable social enterprise that reduces plastic waste, promotes sustainable building innovations, and provides inclusive socio-economic benefits. In addition to the textual analysis, we provide a visual representation of the company's journey in Figure 31.

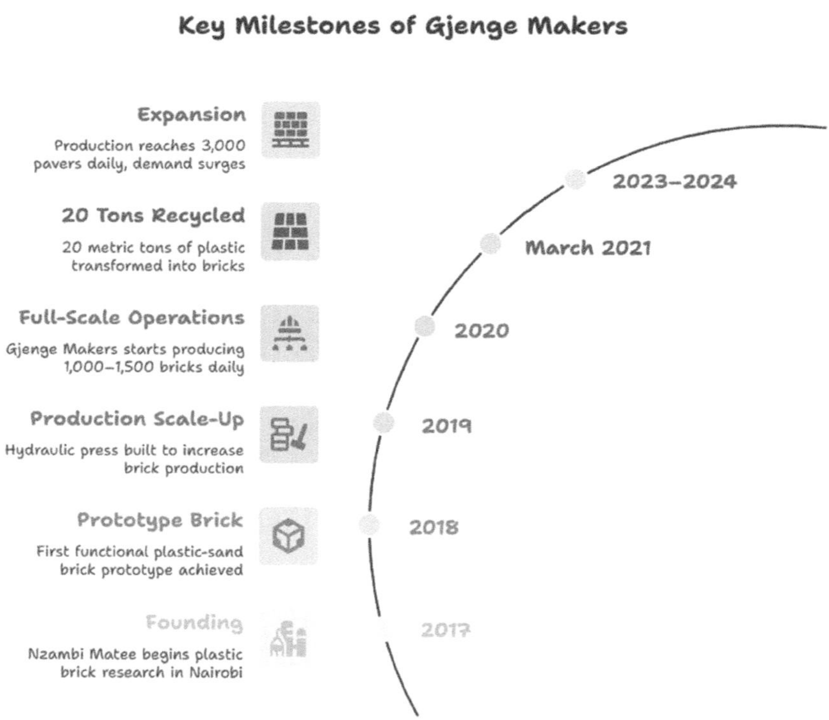

Figure 31 Journey of Gjenge Makers

Source: Created by Author by using Napkin.AI (https://www.napkin.ai/)

Navigating the Path to Sustainability

When Nzambi Matee founded Gjenge Makers in 2017, she was motivated by a strong vision: to transform the growing amounts of plastic waste in Nairobi into something useful. However, the journey was not easy. The first major challenge was the lack of technology to process the mixed plastic waste coming from Nairobi. Instead of giving up, Matee built her own machines. "We decided to do it ourselves. We bought parts from local scrapyards and welded them together," she explained (SWE, 2021; Tuko-KE, 2021). They developed a unique system that included an extruder and a hydraulic press to mold plastic and sand into durable bricks (Reuters, 2021).

Even with a working prototype, there was significant public doubt about the reliability of plastic bricks. The company made no sales in its first year (Nation, 2021). But the team knew their product was strong. Their pavers turned out to be three to seven times stronger than traditional concrete and cheaper as well. They focused on real-world demonstrations, sidewalks, driveways, and school grounds – to show that the bricks could withstand the test of time (Euronews, 2023). Funding was another challenge. At first, few believed in their vision, and most investors kept their distance. However, Matee applied to global innovation challenges and eventually won the UNEP Young Champions of the Earth award in 2020, which helped finance and validate their work (UNEP, 2020). This recognition opened doors to more grants, partnerships, and mentorship from organizations that supported sustainable innovation.

As their product gained popularity, sourcing raw materials became an issue. Nairobi generates a lot of waste, but consistently accessing it required working with local waste pickers and informal networks. Gjenge addressed this by partnering with community collectors and creating supply chains that provided both materials and jobs (Euronews, 2023). Scaling operations presented yet another challenge. As awareness and demand grew, they began producing 3,000 bricks daily but were receiving orders for over 10,000. Instead of stretching their resources too thin, they focused on improving their processes and training more workers, particularly youth and women from disadvantaged communities (Atlas of the Future, 2022).

Matee also had to face gender bias in the male-dominated fields of engineering and entrepreneurship. She turned this challenge into an opportunity by making it part of Gjenge's mission to hire and empower women, demonstrating that sustainable innovation can be both inclusive and effective (Tuko-KE, 2021). Each challenge forced Gjenge Makers to innovate, evolve, and stay focused on their mission. Today, the company is not only a solution to plastic waste but also a symbol of how resourcefulness, community involvement, and determination can create meaningful, lasting change.

4.10 Releaf Papers

> **"It's so obvious that paper can be made from leaves, as the leaf is part of the tree, the main material for papermaking" Releaf Paper**
>
> (Matthis, **2024)**

Overview

Releaf Paper is a young company built on a simple idea: turning fallen leaves into paper. Instead of cutting down more trees, it uses the leaves that nature already provides. The company was founded in 2021 by Ukrainian entrepreneur Valentyn Frechka. When the war in Ukraine began, the team had to move, which made their early journey difficult. In 2022, they shifted their operations to France, where they found support and stability. With help from the European Union, Releaf Paper has now opened its first large factory near Paris. There, they turn city leaf waste into strong paper fibers, offering an alternative to tree pulp, reducing deforestation and creating a more circular, less wasteful system. Figure 32 provides a quick reference to the business overview of Releaf Papers Company.

Need Addressed

Releaf Paper works on two important environmental issues: the growing problem of green waste in cities and the need for eco-friendly raw materials in the paper and packaging industries. Every year, millions of tons of falling leaves wind up in landfills or are burned, which makes the air dirty. At the same time, making paper the old-fashioned way uses a lot of wood pulp, which speeds up deforestation and harms ecosystems. Releaf Paper solves two problems at once by turning fallen leaves, which are a plentiful and renewable resource, into high-quality paper fibers. It cuts down on trash and pollution in cities and puts less stress on trees. This new idea not only helps cities manage their waste in a way that is good for the environment, but it also gives businesses eco-friendly options for packaging, which is in line with the ideas of a circular economy.

Mission Statement

Releaf Paper's goal is to turn fallen leaves into high-quality, long-lasting paper products that may be used again and again. The company wants to maintain forests, stop deforestation, and support a completely circular economy by using less traditional wood pulp. Releaf Paper is all about turning what cities often throw away into a useful resource. It helps cities deal with green trash in a responsible way and gives businesses eco-friendly packaging options that fit with a greener, more sustainable future.

Releaf Papers: The Circular Economy Model

Founded: 2021
Leading Organisation: Releaf Papers
Headquarters: Started in Ukraine and then moved to France
Issue Addressed: Reducing wood pulp usage by making paper with fallen leaves

Mission: Development of aesthetically pleasing and sustainable alternative construction products by using the plastic waste and also generating employment opportunities for the youth and women.

Technology : Patented technology of processing fallen leaves info fibers
Business Model: Circular economy model mainly focusing on B2B (Selling sustainable packaging products (paper bags, boxes, mailers, notebooks) made from fallen leaves).)

Value Proposition: Releaf Paper offers sustainable packaging solutions—paper bags, mailers, gift boxes, notebooks, and custom B2B designs—all made from fallen leaves.

Revenue Streams: Generates revenue through B2B sales of sustainable packaging, custom solutions, municipal partnerships, and innovation grants.

SDGs Addressed: SDG9*, SDG11*, SDG12* , SDG13*, SDG15* , SDG17*,

Results

Environmental outcomes [From Inception till July 2025]:
- ✓ Co2 emission reduced and only emitted just 0.066 kg CO2 per kg i.e. 70–78% lower than traditional paper production.
- ✓ Eliminates the need to cut trees. Estimates suggest saving ~17 trees per ton of paper.

Social outcomes [From Inception till July 2025]:
- ✓ Creates green jobs in waste collection and processing.
- ✓ Reduces urban waste and promotes cleaner cities.

Overview
Releaf Papers founded in 2021 by biotechnologist Valentyn Frechka and entrepreneur Oleksandr (Alexander) is an innovative, France-based (originally Ukraine-founded) company offering a circular economy solution by converting urban green waste specifically fallen leaves—into eco-friendly paper and packaging. Releaf uses a patented mix of mechanical, thermo-chemical, and drying methods to convert leaves into cellulose fibers.. Fibers feed into contracted mills either as standalone fiber or blended with recycled or virgin pulp to make packaging like boxes, bags, mailers, and notebooks

Key Stakeholders
Key stakeholders of Releaf Paper include founders Valentyn Frechka & Oleksandr Sobolenko, clients like Chanel, L'Oréal, Samsung, and municipal partners providing leaf waste. The European Innovation Council (funding), manufacturing partners, and environmental NGOs supporting circular impact.

Challenges:
1. Moving from a small, student-led science project to an industrial-scale manufacturing line capable of producing commercial quantities of leaf-based paper.
2. Ensuring a consistent and clean supply of urban fallen leaves within a limited radius, managing seasonal availability, and maintaining leaf quality for production.
3. Convincing established brands to trust and adopt an entirely new, unconventional raw material for packaging.

Key Success Factors:
1. Invested years in R&D to develop proprietary technology for drying, granulating, and pulping leaves and Secured €2.5M funding from the European Innovation Council to finance scale-up
2. Partnered closely with municipalities (e.g., Paris) to collect leaves sustainably and locally and also developed leaf pre-treatment processes (drying, granulating) to allow storage and year-round production.
3. Built strong partnerships with brands like Chanel, L'Oréal, Samsung by offering pilot runs and certifications.

Source: Releaf Paper. (n.d.). *Releaf Paper – manufacturer of paper made from fallen leaves*. https://www.releaf-paper.com/
SDG 9 – Industry, Innovation and Infrastructure , SDG 11 – Sustainable Cities and Communities , SDG 12 – Responsible Consumption and Production, SDG 13 – Climate Action, SDG 15 – Life on Land, SDG 17 – Partnerships for the Goals

Figure 32 Profile of Releaf Papers: Key Highlights

Source: Created by Author

Where It All Began: The Journey of Releaf Papers

The story of Releaf Paper began in 2017, when Valentyn Frechka, a sixteen-year-old Ukrainian biotechnologist, started working on the idea of manufacturing handmade paper from fallen leaf fibers in his home lab (Elsässer, 2025). What started out as a strange experiment quickly turned into something that showed genuine promise and led to more research into how leaves could be used as a different kind of raw material for creating paper.

Valentyn's journey really began when he was a student at the Junior Academy of Sciences in the Zakarpattia area of Ukraine. Initially, his studies concentrated on agricultural leftovers like flax and straw; however, his concentration gradually transitioned to fallen leaves. This change wasn't a random or silly choice; it happened after months of meticulous testing and a deep connection to nature. His research showed that leaf fibers were good for manufacturing paper, which led to the creation of Releaf Paper. In 2021, Releaf Paper was formally started, with Valentyn as co-founder and head of technology. The corporation moved its research and development work to France as the project progressed. After six years of hard work at a facility in Grenoble, they came up with a proven process that can separate fibers from fallen leaves to make paper (Elsässer, 2025).

Under the direction of CEO and co-founder Oleksandr Sobolenko, the company's growth sped up. The team worked together to successfully test Releaf Paper's first products in numerous EU nations. This led to the opening of the company's first large-scale pilot manufacturing plant near Paris in 2024. This was a big step in turning what started out as a school project into a business strategy that could work.

The proprietary technique from Releaf Paper is known for being very flexible. It uses mechanical, heat, and chemical treatments all at once, so it may be used on more than just fallen leaves in cities. Successful tests have been done with more than just leaves. They have also worked with agricultural waste including pineapple leaves, palm fronds, grape stems, and even flowers. This flexibility lets the company make a lot of eco-friendly products, such as fillers, fibers, paperboards, containerboards, sanitary papers, and bioplastics. At this time, fillers made by mechanical processing are already being made on a large scale. In the meantime, fibers made from thermo-chemical treatment are almost ready for mass production. This technique, which has many parts, makes sure that different kinds of green waste are used to their fullest potential and gives the paper and packaging industries eco-friendly options. It shows that Releaf Paper is still dedicated to being innovative, eco-friendly, and responsible for the environment.

Figure 33 shows the company's journey in a picture, in addition to this story.

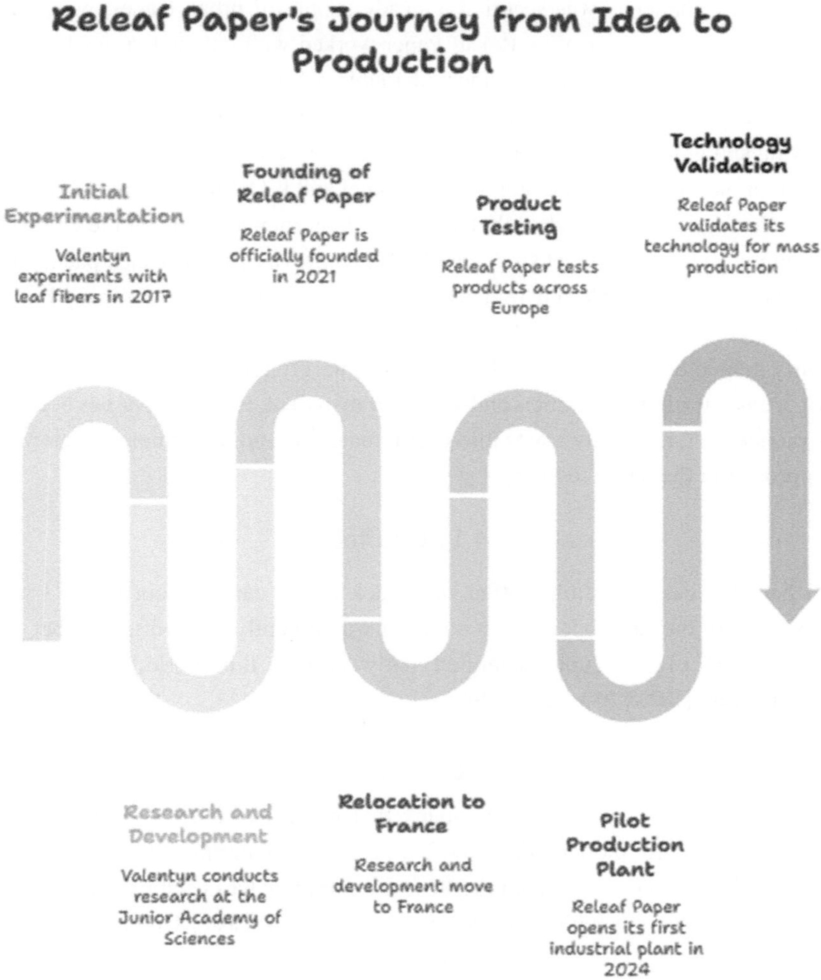

Figure 33 Journey of Releaf Paper

Source: Created by Author by using Napkin.AI (https://www.napkin.ai/)

Challenges and Key Success Factors

Releaf Paper's journey from a school science project to the industrial fallen leaf paper plant has been long and challenging. Each difficulty it faced helped the company grow.

One major challenge was moving its leaf to paper process from the lab to a real factory. Co founder Valentyn Frechka shared that it took years of research and heavy investment in new machines to turn fallen leaves into good quality paper at a large scale. A grant of 2.5 million euros from the European Innovation Council made this possible, and the first factory in France is set to open in 2024.

Another challenge was securing a steady supply of urban leaves, which are seasonal and vary in quality. Releaf Paper worked with city authorities to solve this. As Frechka explained, working with municipalities such as Paris helped them create a model where city waste becomes a resource. The company also developed drying and granulating methods so that leaves can be stored and used all year.

Winning the trust of big brands like Chanel and L'Oréal was equally important. Co-founder Oleksandr Sobolenko said their clients' focus on the environment pushed them to meet strict standards and prove that leaf-based packaging can be both responsible and high performing. On top of this, the company had to handle regulations and certifications. Getting eco labels and other approvals early helped build confidence. By securing smart funding, working with cities, rigorously testing its products and staying transparent, Releaf Paper has become a pioneer in turning city waste into useful materials and in promoting a circular approach in the paper industry.

4.11 Cupffee

"I had the idea for edible coffee cups back in my early school years. I was inspired by the fact that a green solution was urgently needed to combat the billions of plastic cups generated daily around the world," **Miroslav Zapryanov (BBM Magazine, 2022)**

Overview

Cupffee is a Bulgarian-based company that makes sustainable packaging by producing edible, biodegradable coffee cups from natural grains such as oat bran and wheat flour. Founded in 2014, the company was established to tackle the global issue of single-use plastic and paper cup waste. Unlike traditional disposable cups, Cupffee's products are crunchy, heat-resistant (up to 85 °C), leak-proof for hours, and completely edible (Bate, 2022). They offer a zero-waste alternative for both hot and cold beverages.

The company uses a fully automated, zero-waste production process powered by Industry 4.0 technology and operates from a modern facility in Plovdiv, Bulgaria. Leftover production material is repurposed into edible stirrers, supporting its circular economy approach.

Cupffee has expanded to over fufty-five countries and collaborates with major global brands like Lavazza, Etihad Airways, and Lidl. It has received recognition from the European Innovation Council and Horizon 2020 for its focus on sustainable innovation. The company combines food technology with environmental responsibility to change how the world views disposable packaging. Figure 34 provides a quick reference to the business overview of Cupfee Company.

Cupfee: The Circular Economy Model

Founded: 2014
Leading Organisation: Cupfee
Headquarters: :Bulgaria, Europe
Issue Addressed: Plastic and paper cups cause environmental harm through pollution and waste; edible cups provide a sustainable, zero-waste alternative that is biodegradable and safe to consumer.

Mission: To transform disposable coffee culture and drive sustainable change in food industry, one cupfee at a time

Technology : Industry 4.0 automation, Custom Machinery and Specialised recipe

Business Model: Circular economy model mainly focusing on B2B offering to company across the EU, Middle East, Australia and US.

Value Proposition: Offers an innovative, eco-friendly alternative to disposable cups by providing edible, biodegradable coffee cups that are tasty, leak-proof, and safe for the environment..

Revenue Streams: Generates revenue through B2B bulk sales to cafes, airlines, retailers, enterprises.

SDGs Addressed: SDG8*, SDG9*, SDG12* , SDG13*, SDG14*, SDG15* ,

Results

Environmental outcomes [From Inception till July 2025]:
- ✓ Saved ~277,000 kg of CO_2 emissions by replacing single-use cups globally
- ✓ Reducing plastic cup use, they help prevent **marine pollution** and **landfill waste**.

Social outcomes [From Inception till July 2025]:
- ✓ Cupffee creates green jobs in sustainable manufacturing and food tech.
- ✓ Encourages zero-waste lifestyles and raises consumer awareness on plastic pollution.

Overview

Cupffee is a Bulgarian company that produces **edible, biodegradable coffee cups** made from natural grains like wheat and oats. Their innovative cups are fully automated in production, leak-proof, heat-resistant up to 85°C, and designed to replace single-use plastic and paper cups. By offering a zero-waste, tasty alternative, Cupffee helps reduce plastic pollution and promotes sustainable consumption. They partner with major brands like Lavazza and Etihad Airways and distribute their products internationally, supporting green jobs and eco-friendly innovation

Key Stakeholders

Key stakeholders of Cupfee are Suppliers and vendors (Supply raw materials (natural grains, oils) and specialized machinery, ensuring timely delivery and quality), Business clients, end consumers, Investors and financial partners

Challenges:
1. Challenge to create a edible cup that needed to be strong, edible, leak-proof, and tasty at the same time
2. Lack of Suitable Manufacturing Equipment that support their production process
3. Difficulty in Scaling Production i.e. From small batches to industrial-scale while maintaining quality.
4. Developing food-safe, scalable edible products is expensive
5. Reluctance to eat a "cup" and doubts about hygiene and safety

Key Success Factors:
1. Years of R&D to develop a patented recipe using natural grains with no coatings or additives. Resulted in a cup that holds hot liquids for 40 minutes, tastes neutral, and is fully edible.
2. Developed Custom Machinery based on Industry 4.0 principles including custom forming, baking, and packaging lines and partnered with equipment providers like Bühler and König, tailoring the tech for edible cups.
3. Built a fully automated smart factory in Bulgaria capable of producing 3 million cups/month, scalable to 10 million. Automated quality checks and efficient logistics help maintain consistency.
4. Secured strategic investments and built brand partnerships with major global players (e.g., Lavazza, Etihad) to support funding and growth.
5. Launched awareness campaigns and partnered with trusted brands to build credibility. Provided free trials at events and branded promotions to normalize the product.

Source: **Cupffee. (n.d.).** *Home.* https://www.cupffee.me/en/
SDG 8– Decent Work & Economic Growth , SDG 9 – Industry, Innovation and Infrastructure ,SDG 12 – Responsible Consumption and Production, SDG 13 – Climate Action, SDG14- Life Below Water , SDG 15 – Life on Land

Figure 34 Profile of Cupffee: Key Highlights

Source: Created by Author

Need Addressed

The world is facing a growing crisis with single-use plastic and paper cup waste. Billions of disposable cups end up in landfills and oceans every year. Traditional paper cups often have plastic linings, which makes them hard to recycle and adds to long-term environmental problems. Consumers and businesses are looking for eco-friendly, practical, and safe options that don't sacrifice convenience. Cupffee responds to this urgent need by providing a 100 percent edible, biodegradable cup. This product eliminates waste by turning a typically discarded item into something sustainable and consumable. It meets both environmental concerns and user expectations for functionality, hygiene, and taste.

Mission Statement

To revolutionize single-use consumption by creating sustainable, edible alternatives that eliminate waste, inspire responsible habits, and protect the planet – one cup at a time.

Where It All Began: The Journey of Cupffee

Cupffee started as a personal mission. Founder Miroslav Zapryanov was inspired by the large amount of plastic waste created by coffee shops in his hometown. He wondered if there was a better way, one that could tackle both convenience and sustainability (Southey, 2023). After years of testing, this vision became Cupffee: a biodegradable, edible wafer cup made from just seven natural ingredients, including oat bran, wheat flour, sugar, and oil.

The company was established in 2014 and moved from concept to industrial production in 2018. They turned their unique recipe into a manufacturable product. Designed for both hot and cold drinks, Cupffee's cups can handle temperatures up to 85 °C, stay crunchy for about 40 minutes, and remain leak-proof for up to 12 hours (Southey, 2023). This addresses important performance issues for edible packaging (Bate, 2022).

To make this idea a reality, Cupffee invested in smart manufacturing. Their operations in Plovdiv, Bulgaria, use fully automated production lines equipped for Industry 4.0. These lines cover mixing, dough-making, forming, baking, and packaging, using customized machines from industry leaders like Bühler and König Cupffee. Scaling production allowed them to grow internationally. Today, Cupffee ships to fifty-five countries and serves over 353 clients. They claim to have avoided 277,000 kg of CO_2 emissions, demonstrating the real-world environmental benefits of their innovation Cupffee (Southey, 2023).

To further support technological and market growth, Cupffee received a €1.3 million grant from the European Innovation Council (EIC) and

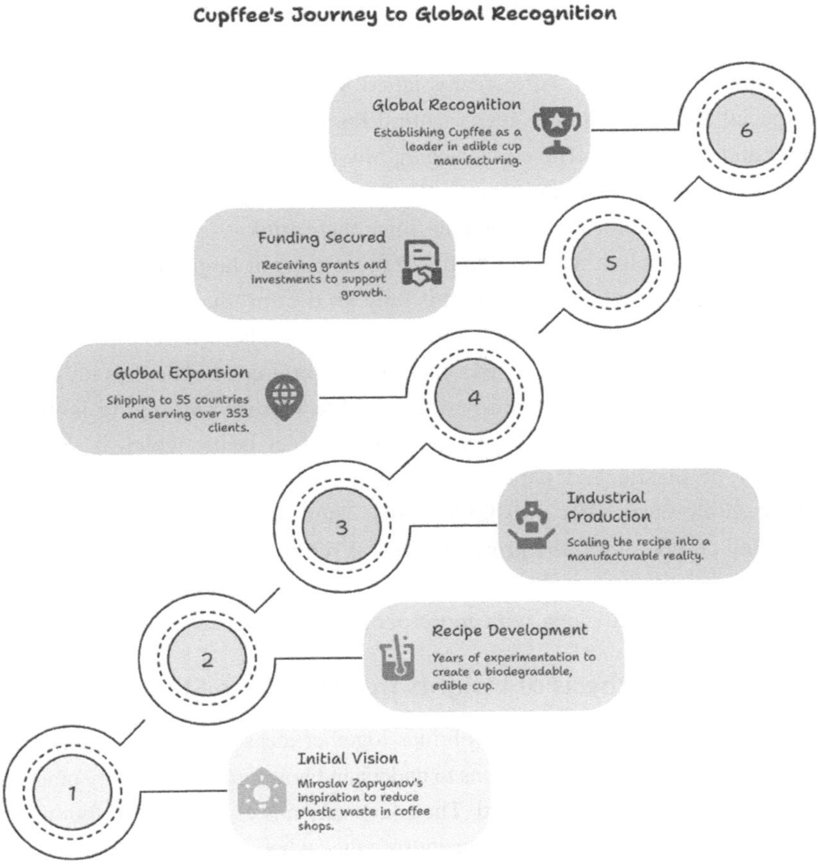

Figure 35 Journey of Cupffee

Source: Created by Author by using Napkin.AI (https://www.napkin.ai/)

€500,000 in pre-seed investment led by Eleven Ventures (Southey, 2023). This funding helped them move from lab prototypes to large-scale production, strengthening Cupffee's ability to become a leader in edible cup and stirrer manufacturing FoodNavigator.com. Through inspiration, technical skill, sustainable manufacturing, and strategic growth, Cupffee has transformed from a dream into a well-known brand. It is changing the disposable cup industry with edible, zero-waste solutions. In addition to the textual analysis, we provide a visual representation of the company's journey in Figure 35.

Navigating the Path to Sustainability

Cupffee is a young company from Bulgaria that set out to do something very unusual: make coffee cups that you can actually eat. The idea sounded simple, but turning it into reality was not easy. Their first big challenge was the cup itself. It had to be safe to eat, strong enough to hold hot drinks and stay crisp without getting soggy. After many failed attempts, the team finally created a special recipe using only seven natural ingredients, such as oat bran, wheat flour and coconut oil. The cup is vegan, low in calories and can hold drinks as hot as a normal coffee. It stays crunchy for about forty minutes, which is more than enough time for most people to finish their drink.

The next problem was how to make these cups in large numbers. Regular food machines could not handle this new kind of product. Instead of giving up, Cupffee designed its own production line. The whole process, from mixing the dough to baking and packing, is automated. There is no factory waste. Even extra dough is turned into edible stirrers, so nothing is thrown away. Cupffee also wanted to respond to a larger issue, which is the huge number of plastic and paper cups that are used once and then dumped. Their edible cups offer a different path. They do not need to be recycled and they do not add to the growing piles of rubbish. Support from European and national funding programs has helped the company grow and share this simple but powerful idea with more people and businesses.

5 Synthesis of Insights from the Case Studies

The analysis of the selected cases brings together ideas from recent studies and examples from global organizations to understand how circular economy practices are actually built in the real world. The conversation is organized into four parts.

First, it looks at the problems businesses face when they try to adopt circular solutions. Second, it describes the actions they took to overcome these hurdles. Third, it highlights the circular strategies hidden within those actions. Finally, it uses the EXIST framework to place these lessons in the wider picture of long term circular change. The stories of the eleven businesses studied show that building a circular economy in developing regions is both full of hope and full of difficulty. Each business began with a clear purpose, such as turning waste into useful products, finding better materials, or changing daily buying habits. As they grew, they ran into real world barriers, such as lack of awareness, weak systems, or unclear rules. This shows that even the most creative ideas must wrestle with practical challenges.

To organize these lessons, this study uses what it calls the Challenge and Action Framework. It connects common problems for circular businesses, such as low customer awareness, lack of funding, difficulty in scaling, strong competition, technical barriers, and regulatory risks, with the concrete steps firms took in response. For example, Phool worked directly with temple communities to build trust and demand for their products. Algramo questioned long standing habits around single use packaging by introducing refillable options. Attero learned to navigate India's complex e-waste rules so the firm could grow and gain legitimacy. Many companies faced similar problems, but each found its own way forward, shaped by local conditions and people.

The EXIST framework then helps us see the deeper patterns behind these actions. It does not replace the Challenge and Action view, but adds a wider system perspective. Through this lens, several types of circular strategies become visible. Some businesses reduced resource use, like Gjenge Makers, which turned plastic waste into strong bricks. Others slowed resource flows, like Ecocitex, which turned discarded clothes into yarn. Some encouraged new habits, like Cupffee, which created edible and compostable cups to support more thoughtful consumption. Together, these examples show how different strategies can combine to push a system toward circularity.

The analysis also underlines the role of skills and knowledge. Craste learned how to convert crop waste into packaging. Releaf Paper developed new ways to make pulp from fallen leaves. These cases show that innovation often rests on strong technical ability and problem-solving skills. Equally important is collaboration. In every case, change depended on different actors working together. Algramo's progress was closely tied to partnerships with local shops and public institutions. Attero's growth was deeply linked to changes in Indian regulation. These stories show that partnerships are not a bonus but a basic requirement for circular progress.

Finally, this discussion reminds us that success in a circular economy cannot be measured by profit alone. The idea of Circular Value Performance (CVP) points out that social and environmental results matter just as much. Ecocitex's early financial struggles show how hard it can be to balance long-term economic survival with broader goals. Yet the company's persistence shows that value is more than earnings on a balance sheet. Putting the Challenge and Action Framework together with the EXIST framework reveals a fuller picture of circular entrepreneurship in emerging economies. The first shows what entrepreneurs face and how they respond. The second explains why those responses matter for larger system change. Building circular businesses in such settings is not just about bringing in new technologies. It means rethinking business models for contexts with limited resources, dealing with uneven and changing policies, and working within tightly woven social systems. In this journey, trust, partnerships, and resilience matter just as much as new ideas and technical solutions.

5.1 Common Challenges on the Basis of Analysis

The journey of the eleven circular economy startups examined in this study reveals a striking pattern: though they operate in vastly different contexts and industries ranging from floral waste management in India to edible coffee cups in Bulgaria, they all encounter remarkably similar systemic challenges. These challenges span from consumer awareness and funding shortages to technological barriers and regulatory uncertainties. Yet, what is perhaps most compelling is how each company has responded with creativity, persistence, and community-driven strategies, offering valuable lessons for the broader sustainability and entrepreneurship ecosystem. Please refer to Table 5 for more details about the challenges and supporting facts.

Table 5 Case-Based Evidence of Challenges Encountered by Circular Startups

Key challenges	Stage	Supporting facts
Limited consumer awareness and behavior change	Early & Growth	**Phool (2017):** *"It was difficult to convince them. Flowers offered at temples hold deep religious significance, so naturally, there was hesitation . . . They wanted to know why I wanted the flowers and what exactly I intended to do with them." (Ankit Agarwal, Founder) (Nabi, 2025)* **Attero (2008):** *"The problem is collection of e-waste . . . Almost 98 per cent of the e-waste recycling is done in the unorganized sector. Lack of awareness is the main cause of this." – Nitin Gupta, CEO. (Suneja, 2013)* **Ecocitex (2020):** *"We have to educate people that recycling has a cost and that donating clothes is not the same as recycling." – Rosario Hevia, Founder (Miliani, 2022)* ***Africa Collect Textiles (2013):*** *"People thought we were crazy when we started collecting old clothes." – Daniël Kloos, Co-Founder (Africa Collect Textiles, 2025)*
Funding and investment constraints	Early & Growth	**Phool (2017):** *"When we started out, they had an investment of only ₹72,000 . . . they managed to scale only when they received*

Table 5 (cont.)

Key challenges	Stage	Supporting facts
		support from IIT Kanpur's start-up incubation and innovation centre." (Sinha, 2025) **Attero (2008):** *"We spent $2 million for land/ building and approximately $2.5 million for machinery . . . Challenges were faced at multiple levels . . . Getting all the required licences also took over a year." – Nitin Gupta, Co-founder (Gupta, 2012)* **Ecocitex (2020):** *"Ecocitex is loss-making during its first three years of operation . . . receives more clothes than it recycles and recycles more than it sells." – Co-founder, reflecting pressure on working capital (Gómez, 2023).* **Gjenge Makers (2017):** *"I shut down my social life for a year, and put all my savings into this." – Nzambi Matee, Founder (WA Contents, 2021)*
Production and scaling challenges	Growth	**Gjenge Makers (2017):** "*The demand is greater than the production capacity . . . at 1,500 bricks per day." – Nzambi Matee, Founder.* **Phool (2017):** Temple flowers arrive mixed with leaves/plastic, vary by season, and can contain toxins – tough for consistent, higher-volume production (UNESCO, 2021). **Fortuna Cools (2018):** Turning coconut husks into uniform insulation/coolers at scale requires local fiber processing, QA, and reliable farmer partnerships across islands (Trahant, 2021) **Ecocitex (2020)**: Textile-to-yarn recycling needs heavy spinning/cleaning lines; Ecocitex also faced a factory fire that destroyed machinery and inventory, complicating scale (Coombe, 2023). **Cupfee (2014):** To serve airlines/cafés at scale, Cupffee needed high-throughput,

Table 5 (cont.)

Key challenges	Stage	Supporting facts
		consistent lines and stabilized product properties (Kostadinova, 2023). **Releaf Paper (2021)**: Making paper from fallen leaves demands new fiber prep lines and plant financing; the Ukraine war forced relocation/continuity plans.
Market competition and pricing pressures	Growth & Maturity	**Phool (2017):** Competes with inexpensive incense and synthetic leather, making pricing a hurdle (UNFCCC, 2018). **Fortuna Cools (2018):** Cheaper Styrofoam coolers dominate market; produces higher-cost coconut husk alternatives (Peters, 2019). **Salubata (2020):** Upcycled-plastic shoes must compete with synthetic, cost-effective footwear (Ihekire, 2021). **Algramo (2013)**: Consumers expect ultra-low prices on single-use packs; refill often perceived as inconvenient or more expensive (Peters, 2020).
Technological and process barriers	Growth	**Phool (2017):** Phool faced the technological challenge of converting temple flower waste into hygienic, scalable biomaterials. Developing Fleather, a leather alternative made from mycelium, required extensive R&D to stabilize texture and durability (UNESCO, 2021) **Attero (2008):** Attero's biggest technological barrier was setting up an integrated e-waste recycling and refining system in India, which required expensive specialized machinery and regulatory licenses. Nitin Gupta explained: "We spent \$2 million for land/building and approximately \$2.5 million for machinery . . . Getting all the required licences also took over a year." (Gupta, 2012, as cited in YourStory).

Table 5 (cont.)

Key challenges	Stage	Supporting facts
		Fortuna Cools (2018): Fortuna Cools struggled to replace Styrofoam with natural fiber insulation that could withstand cold-chain logistics. The team co-created "Nutshell Coolers" with farmers by developing coconut-fiber insulation and testing durability under field conditions before scaling manufacturing (Causeartist, 2020). **Ecocitex (2020)** The main barrier was technological: how to spin yarn from textile waste without water, dyes, or chemicals. (Coombe, 2023)

5.1.1 Limited Consumer Awareness and Behavior Change

Many of these firms first had to create a market before they could compete in it. People had rarely seen products such as Phool's incense made from temple flowers, Cupffee's edible cups or Algramo's refill systems. For most customers, these new products were easily pushed aside by cheaper and more familiar options.

To overcome this, companies invested time in people, not just in products. They raised awareness, told stories and built relationships in the communities where they worked. Phool linked its incense to the idea of cleaning and honouring sacred rivers, giving the product cultural and emotional weight. Algramo showed how its refills could both protect the environment and save money, making new habits feel practical and close to daily life.

These examples show that in a circular economy, helping people understand and feel connected to change is central to the business, not an extra activity. It is not enough to offer eco friendly products. People need to care about them, see how they fit into their lives and feel the benefits of changing their habits

5.1.2 Funding and Investment Constraints

Finding money was a major obstacle. Attero needed large investments to build heavy infrastructure for recycling e-waste. Africa Collect Textiles and Salubata struggled with investors who saw them as risky and untested. Those who moved ahead often relied on different and patient sources of funds, such as impact investors, incubators, public schemes and crowdfunding. These forms of support brought not only capital but also visibility and trust. For circular startups, regular investment ideas do not always apply. Profits may come slowly, while social and environmental benefits appear much sooner. This makes blended and patient finance essential if young circular firms are to survive their early years and grow into solutions that can reach more people.

5.1.3 Production and Scaling Challenges

Growing production while staying sustainable proved demanding. Craste had to design entirely new facilities to turn farm waste into packaging. Gjenge Makers in Kenya struggled to produce enough plastic bricks without access to costly machinery. These stories reveal a basic tension. Many of the best answers for the environment require long periods of testing, investment and learning to work well at scale. To manage this, firms often worked closely with universities, research centres and local communities, increasing capacity step by step. This steady approach helped them expand without losing quality or drifting away from their core purpose.

5.1.4 Market Competition and Pricing Pressures

Creating a sustainable product was only the beginning. The harder task was competing with cheap mass produced goods. Nutshell's natural coolers were compared with low cost plastic versions. Cupffee's edible cups were judged against disposable cups that cost very little. Matching those prices was almost impossible in price sensitive markets. To survive, these firms chose not to compete only on cost. They offered strong designs, durability, playful experiences and stories of responsibility and innovation. By appealing to customers who cared about more than price, they created their own space in the market.

5.1.5 Technological and Process Barriers

Many firms had to invent new processes from the ground up. Releaf Paper worked out how to turn fallen leaves into paper using less energy, something that had not been done before. Salubata created modular shoes without any clear industry example to follow. Such efforts demanded time, research funds and persistence through repeated setbacks. To move ahead, companies often partnered with universities, protected their ideas through patents and reinvested early earnings into further development. Circular startups therefore became testing grounds for new ideas, constantly refining their methods and creating fresh solutions.

5.1.6 Policy, Regulation, and Safety Risks

Government rules helped and hindered at the same time. Attero and Craste benefited from restrictions on burning e-waste and crop residues, yet they still faced gaps and delays. Cupffee and Salubata had to spend long periods securing food safety and product approvals before they could sell widely. Phool received useful backing from government linked incubators, but many others struggled with unclear or shifting rules that made long term planning difficult.

This shows that clear and steady policy is just as important as finance. When regulations change often or are poorly enforced, uncertainty grows. Startups that engage with policymakers and form alliances are better placed to reduce these risks and contribute to fairer, more supportive regulations.

5.1.7 The Power of Community and Partnerships

Community ties were often a lifeline. Africa Collect Textiles relied on local networks to collect used clothes. Gjenge Makers created jobs for women and young people in Nairobi's informal settlements. Phool built its work around temple communities. These partnerships strengthened supply chains, built trust and created a sense of shared ownership. Such efforts show that circular economy projects are about more than managing materials. They aim to build inclusive local systems where environmental gains go hand in hand with social benefits and where communities are active partners, not just end users.

5.2 Challenge-Action Framework

Since we have already discussed the challenges these companies faced, it is equally important to see how they addressed them. To capture this, we have developed the Challenge–Action Framework, presented in the Tables 6 and 7.

5.3 Circular Strategies: Engines of Transition

According to Geissdoerfer et al. (2017)., literature on the circular economy mainly identified three strategies: narrowing (using fewer resources), closing (recycling resources), and slowing (extending lifespans). By including the work of Bocken et al. (2016), our analysis highlights two additional strategies that are particularly relevant in the field of circular economy: regenerating (returning resources to ecological systems) and enabling (creating the infrastructures, platforms, and partnerships that support circularity). On the basis of these five strategies, we have tried to give the framework here. Please refer to Table 8 for more details.

Table 6 Challenge-action framework- summary view

Actions ↓ / Challenges →	Limited consumer awareness & behavior change	Funding & investment constraints	Production & scaling challenges	Market competition & pricing pressures	Technological & process barriers
Raised awareness & built market demand	Phool (2017), Algramo (2013/ 2019), Ecocitex (2018), Fortuna Cools (2020)	Attero (2008), Cupffee (2014), Salubata (2020)	Releaf Paper (2018), Gjenge Makers (2018), Craste (2018)	Fortuna Cools (2020), Algramo (2013/ 2019), Ecocitex (2018)	Cupffee (2014), Releaf Paper (2018), Gjenge Makers (2018), Salubata (2020)
Secured funding & investor support	—	Attero (2008), Cupffee (2014), Algramo (2019), Salubata (2020)	—	—	—
Improved processes & ensured quality standards	Phool (2017)	—	Releaf Paper (2018), Craste (2018)	Fortuna Cools (2020)	Cupffee (2014)
Developed local supply chains & community partnerships	Phool (2017)	—	Africa Collect Textiles (2014), Fortuna Cools (2020), Craste (2018)	Algramo (2013/ 2019), Gjenge Makers (2018)	—

Differentiated products & advocated policy support	Algramo (2013/2019)	—	—	Fortuna Cools (2020), Ecocitex (2018)	Releaf Paper (2018)
Advanced innovation through R&D & technology collaboration	—	—	Craste (2018)	—	Releaf Paper (2018), Gjenge Makers (2018), Salubata (2020)
Engaged in policy, compliance & industry alliances	Phool (2017)	Attero (2008)	—	—	Releaf Paper (2018), Algramo (2019)

Table 7 Challenge-action framework for circular adoption – detailed view

Challenges → / Actions↓	**Limited consumer awareness & behavior change**	**Funding & investment constraints**	**Production & scaling challenges**	**Market competition & pricing pressures**	**Technological & process barriers**
Raised awareness & built market demand	**Phool** went temple-to-temple explaining why throwing sacred flowers in the Ganga harms water; once priests understood, they began giving flower waste directly to the team. *[1]* **Algramo** met NYC shoppers where they buy staples, letting them try reusables without paying more; pilots with retailers gave people a low-friction first experience. *[3][14]* **Ecocitex** talked	**Attero** told investors bluntly that e-waste is a heavy-capex business; Nitin Gupta details the multi-million-dollar site + machinery outlay and the long licensing runway they had to finance. *[2]* **Cupffee** closed a €1.8 m round to move from "great demo" to mass production for cafés and brands. *[6]* **Salubata** won the AfDB/GCA Youth ADAPT grant, using	**Releaf Paper** moved from lab to industry by launching a pilot line in France to prove repeatable, quality leaf-pulp at scale. *[13]* **Gjenge Makers** built and iterated its own presses to achieve consistent, high-throughput paving blocks from mixed plastic – learning by doing on the factory floor. *[8]* **Craste** established moulded-fibre lines that turn farm straw	**Fortuna Cools** positioned coconut-fiber insulation as a like-for-like replacement for cheap foam, competing on performance in hot, humid conditions (fish, vaccines, food) rather than "eco" tags alone. *[7]* **Algramo** countered the "single-use is cheaper" mindset by offering same-or-lower unit prices via smart-dispensing and partnerships	**Cupffee** had to make an edible cup that's leak-proof and pleasant; the team engineered a food-safe, bakery-grade process that stands up to hot drinks without coatings. *[5]* **Releaf Paper** solved for pulping fallen leaves with an energy-lean, chemical-light process adapted to non-wood feedstock. *[12]* **Gjenge Makers** engineered

	openly about why "recycling costs money," correcting the common donor belief that donation = recycling. *[4]* **Fortuna Cools** co-designed coolers with Filipino fishers so users who'd only trusted Styrofoam could experience a natural-fiber alternative that actually worked on the boat. *[7]*	it to patent its modular shoe and grow output. *[11]*	into packaging parts, demonstrating steady runs beyond the lab. *[16]*	with big brands. *[3]* *[14]* **Ecocitex** had to price yarn and upcycled textiles realistically even while receipts of clothing outpaced sales during its first years. *[4]*	a polymer-sand recipe and rugged machinery to turn mixed plastic into bricks that meet strength specs. *[8]* **Salubata** developed a modular shoe platform – one sole, many uppers – requiring its own tooling and assembly know-how. *[10]*
Secured funding & investor support	—	**Attero** raised and deployed heavy capex while navigating year-long licensing, a reality they communicated early to backers. *[2]* **Cupffee**'s 2023	—	—	—

Table 7 (cont.)

Challenges → / Actions↓	**Limited consumer awareness & behavior change**	**Funding & investment constraints**	**Production & scaling challenges**	**Market competition & pricing pressures**	**Technological & process barriers**
		round financed new lines and faster expansion into cafés and CPG. *[6]* **Algramo**'s NYC collaboration came with ecosystem backing (Closed Loop Partners) to de-risk roll-out. *[3]* **Salubata** leveraged grant + accelerator support to ramp from ~100 to 500+ pairs/month. *[11]*			
Improved processes & ensured	**Phool** formalized hygiene/quality protocols so incense and biomaterials	—	**Releaf Paper** validated quality specs with the French pilot so packaging buyers	**Fortuna Cools** proved thermal performance head-to-head vs. foam, building user	**Cupffee** refined baking parameters to balance taste, crunch and heat resistance

quality standards	from temple flowers met consumer and safety expectations. *[1]*		could trust non-wood fibre at industrial standards. *[13]* **Craste**'s moulded-fibre operation standardized on agri-waste inputs while meeting packaging tolerances. *[16]*	trust on quality, not just eco-benefits. *[7]*	without plastic liners – quality by process, not coatings. *[5]*
Developed local supply chains & community partnerships	**Phool** created a dignified supply chain with temple committees and women's groups to funnel florals away from rivers. *[1]*	—	**Africa Collect Textiles** set up city drop-off partners and sorting to capture textiles that previously had no reliable local pathway. *[9]* **Fortuna Cools** sourced husks from coconut processors and partnered in coastal communities to steady fibre supply. *[7]*	**Algramo** partnered with neighborhood stores/brands so refilling felt like a normal errand, not a special trip. *[3]* *[14]*	**Gjenge Makers** worked with Nairobi waste streams and community collectors to secure mixed plastics consistently for bricks. *[8]*

Table 7 (cont.)

Challenges → / Actions↓	Limited consumer awareness & behavior change	Funding & investment constraints	Production & scaling challenges	Market competition & pricing pressures	Technological & process barriers
Differentiated products & advocated policy support	**Algramo** framed reuse as cost-savings and convenience, not sacrifice, helping households switch habits without paying more. *[3]* *[14]*	—	—	**Fortuna Cools** positioned natural-fiber insulation as field-proof and repairable – an everyday, affordable alternative to Styrofoam. *[7]* **Ecocitex** differentiated with truly zero-waste fibre/yarn, not just "second-hand," educating buyers about recycled-textile value. *[4]*	**Releaf Paper** advocates non-wood fibres to meet packaging demand without deforestation, using live industrial demos to make the case. *[12][13]*
Advanced innovation through R&D & technology collaboration	—	—	**Craste**'s R&D unlocked straw-to-pulp and moulding routes that keep silica and contaminants from	—	**Releaf Paper**'s energy-efficient pulping of leaves, **Gjenge Makers**' home-grown extrusion/press line,

			wrecking equipment – enabling stable runs. *[16]*		and **Salubata**'s patented modular platform are all outcomes of sustained in-house R&D, not off-the-shelf kits. *[12][8][10][11]*
Engaged in policy, compliance & industry alliances	**Phool** worked respectfully with religious institutions —critical local governance for waste access and social licence. *[1]*	**Attero** navigated India's e-waste/EPR licensing maze – year-plus paperwork that shaped its financing plan. *[2]*	—	—	**Releaf Paper**'s European pilots and **Algramo**'s retailer coalitions align with tightening packaging/reuse rules, helping each firm stay on the right side of policy while shaping standards. *[13][3][14]*

Sources: (1) (UNESCO), (2) (YourStory, 2022), (3) (Closed Loop Partners, 2020a), (4) (Resource, 2022), (5) (Whitehead, 2021), (6) (Kostadinova, 2023), (7) (Causeartist, 2021), (8) (KEEN Effect, 2021), (9) (Africanews, 2021), (10) (UNC, 2022), (11) (GCA, 2021), (12) (Releaf Paper, 2022), (13) (Releaf Paper, 2023a), (14) (Sustainable Brands, 2020b), (15) (Arthavaan, 2022).

Table 8 The EXIST model for enablers of circular economy implementation

Element	EXIST (Evidence from Cases)
Narrowing	Use of waste- or bio-based alternatives: coconut husk insulation (Fortuna), edible cups (Cupffee), leaf pulp (Releaf).
Closing	Recycling/upcycling of e-waste, plastics, and textiles: Attero, Gjenge, Ecocitex, ACT, Salubata.
Slowing	Reuse and refill models: Algramo's smart dispenser refills reduce single-use packaging.
Regenerating	Organic waste valorization into biomaterials: Phool, Craste, Cupffee, Fortuna.
Enabling	Platforms and partnerships: Attero's MetalMandi/ Selsmart, Algramo's IoT-enabled refills.
Resource Sourcing	Localized feedstock sourcing: temple flowers (Phool), agro-residues (Craste), plastics (Gjenge).
Revalorization Technology	Technologies span mechanical, chemical, biological: Ecocitex (mechanical), Attero (chemical), Phool (bio).
Delivery Models	Diverse delivery: B2B substitution (Craste, Releaf), B2 C branding (Salubata, Cupffee), service (Algramo).
Impact & Metrics	Metrics reported: waste diverted, jobs created, CO_2 avoided – but inconsistent across cases.
Businesses	Innovative but resource-constrained firms integrating local waste streams into business models.
Communities	Communities involved in collection and processing; informal roles critical (ACT, Ecocitex).
Governments/ Finance	Fragmented support; early-stage EPR, sporadic procurement, limited concessional finance.

5.3.1 Narrowing Resource Flows

What Exists: Out of the discussed cases, in some cases we noticed how firms are using the renewable and waste based inputs instead of using some new resources. Fortuna Cools transforms coconut husks, a by-product often burned, into insulation panels for coolers. Cupffee produces edible coffee cups that reduce single-use plastic or paper waste. Releaf Paper turns fallen leaves into paper pulp, decreasing deforestation.

The crux: Narrowing plays important role when new material imports are costly or unreliable. By reducing reliance on resource-intensive inputs, these firms are trying to enhance both environmental resilience and supply security.

5.3.2 Closing Resource Loops

What exists: Although in all the discussed cases, founders have tried to use this concept of closing resource loops but in some cases it has been followed more diligently, like Attero (India) shows advanced e-waste recycling, recovering precious metals while digitizing informal scrap flows. Gjenge Makers (Kenya) turns plastic waste into durable paving bricks. Ecocitex (Chile) and ACT (Kenya/Nigeria) convert discarded textiles into yarn or upcycled clothing. Salubata (Nigeria) makes modular shoe soles from plastic waste.

• The crux: Closing loops in developing economies often tackles the combined issues of waste mismanagement and material scarcity. These efforts demonstrate how "waste" can serve as a reliable feedstock if processes are formalized.

5.3.3 Slowing Resource Loops

What exists: There are some cases in which founders have focused on increasing the lifespan of the existing product such as Algramo (Chile) which extends the lifecycle of packaging by allowing refills at smart dispensers. This not only cuts down on packaging waste but also makes consumer goods more affordable through pay-per-use.

The crux: Slowing focuses less on material substitution and more on changing consumer habits. In low-income areas, it addresses affordability, accessibility, and sustainability at the same time.

5.3.4 Regenerating Systems

What exists: Phool (India) turns floral waste into incense and biomaterials (e.g., "Fleather"), preventing river pollution and creating new industries. Craste (India) processes agricultural residues into boards and packaging, reducing stubble burning and its air pollution effects. Cupffee's edible cups and Fortuna's fiber-based boards also help ecosystems by replacing unsustainable packaging with biodegradable alternatives.

The crux: Regeneration is especially important in emerging economies, where waste streams often harm ecosystems directly. By converting waste into regenerative products, these firms not only lessen damage but also create positive ecological feedback loops.

5.3.5 Enabling Ecosystems

What exists: Attero's platforms (MetalMandi, Selsmart) and Algramo's IoT-enabled dispensers illustrate how enabling infrastructures (digital, logistical, institutional) can organize flows and influence behavior. Corporate partnerships (like Unilever with Algramo and Ripley with Ecocitex) also show effective collaborations.

The crux: Enabling acts as the "hidden strategy" behind circular transitions it ensures that practices at the firm level become widespread. Without these enablers, innovations often remain isolated and fragile.

5.4 Value-Chain Capabilities: Building Blocks of Circularity

Beyond strategies, ventures need to develop capabilities throughout the value chain. These capabilities are sourcing, revalorization technology, delivery models, and impact measurement. These act as the "operational ring" of the framework.

5.4.1 Resource Sourcing

What exists: Each firm bases its model on locally available feedstock. Phool sources temple flowers; ACT and Ecocitex use textile waste; Gjenge collects discarded plastics; Craste processes agricultural residues. Locality defines feasibility.

The crux: In developing economies, the location of feedstock and its accessibility matter more than advanced technology. A business cannot thrive without reliable input.

5.4.2 Revalorization Technology

What exists: The cases include mechanical (Ecocitex), chemical (Attero), biological (Phool), and hybrid technologies (Craste, Cupffee). These show how waste can be transformed into market-grade inputs.

The crux: Technology changes how we see things, shifting from "waste" to "valuable resource." However, without quality benchmarking, recycled or bio-based products often get stuck in "low trust" categories.

5.4.3 Delivery Models

What exists: Models range from B2B substitution (Craste boards) to B2 C branding (Salubata shoes, Cupffee cups) to service innovations (Algramo refills). Delivery formats influence how value is captured.

The crux: In emerging markets, delivery must find a balance between affordability and trust. Many ventures gain traction by aligning circularity with cost savings or access benefits.

5.4.4 Impact and Metrics

What exists: Companies report the tons of waste diverted, jobs created, or CO_2 avoided. However, the reporting is inconsistent and fragmented.

The crux: Without a consistent way to measure, circularity might be seen as just anecdotal or "boutique."

5.5 Actor Triad: Who Drives Circular Transitions

Circular economy transitions don't just depend on firms. They need coordinated efforts across businesses, communities, and governments/financiers.

Businesses: Should integrate multiple strategies, invest in reverse logistics, and focus on inclusivity. They drive innovation but need partners to scale.

Communities: Serve as both suppliers (like informal waste pickers, farmers) and beneficiaries (through jobs and income). Their engagement and legitimacy are key for sustainability.

Governments and Financiers: Create the supportive environment through EPR policies, green procurement, concessional finance, and infrastructure. They act as catalysts at the system level.

5.6 EXIST Framework

The EXIST Circular Transition Framework emphasizes the findings from the 11 case studies into a multi-layered model. It visually represents how circular practices currently operate (EXIST). The framework is structured around **four interconnected layers.** Pictorial representation has been done in Figure 36.

5.6.1 Inner Core: Circular Value Performance (CVP)

At the center of the framework is CVP, which is the main result of circular economy transitions. It mainly includes environmental, social, economic, and systemic dimensions:

- Environmental: waste diverted, CO_2 avoided, new resource reduction.
- Social: inclusive jobs, wages, gender/youth participation.
- Economic: affordability, cost savings, and profitability.
- Systemic: loop closure, traceability, and institutional integration.

Placing CVP at the center highlights that all strategies, capabilities, and participants ultimately contribute to measurable outcomes.

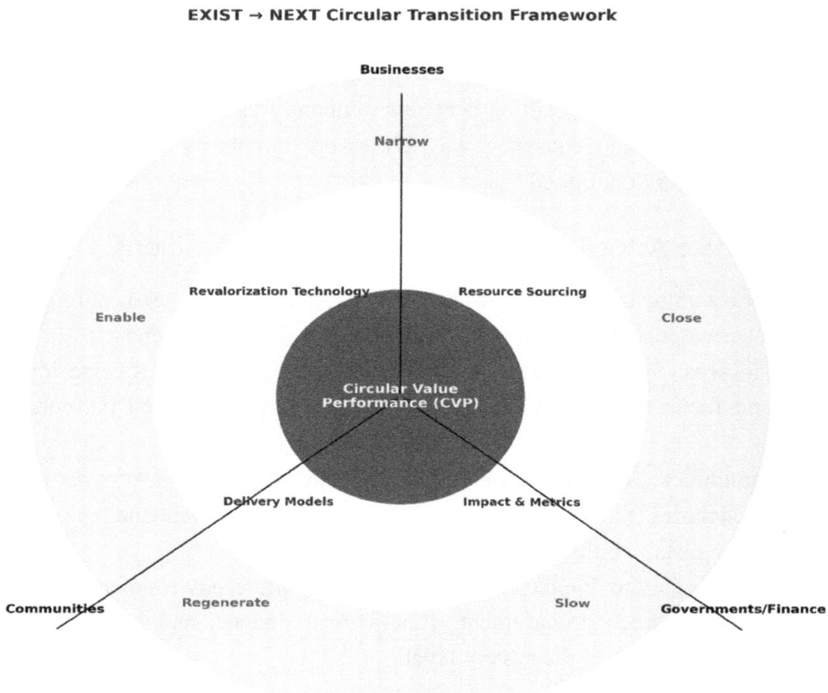

Figure 36 Exist framework

Source: Created by Author

5.6.2 Middle Ring: Value-Chain Capabilities

The four capabilities form the operational core that allows strategies to take shape:

- Resource Sourcing – how firms secure waste streams or biomaterials (e.g., Phool, ACT).
- Revalorization Technology – the processes that transform waste into usable inputs (e.g., Attero's e-waste recovery, Craste's agro-board).
- Delivery Models – business models that bring products and services to markets, from B2B substitution (Craste) to refill services (Algramo).
- Impact & Metrics – measuring outcomes such as jobs created, tons recycled, or CO_2 avoided.

These capabilities sit between strategies and outcomes to highlight their role: firms must build them to turn vision into performance.

5.6.3 Outer Ring: Circular Strategies

Five strategies surround the capabilities. They show how companies implement circularity:

- Narrow (use fewer resources) – for example, Releaf Paper, Fortuna Cools.
- Close (reuse or recycle resources) – for example, Attero, Gjenge Makers, Ecocitex.
- Slow (extend resource lifetimes) – for example, Algramo's refill system.
- Regenerate (restore ecosystems) – for example, Phool, Craste.
- Enable (create infrastructures and partnerships) – for example, Attero's MetalMandi, Algramo's RFID-linked logistics.

The outward position shows that these strategies are the most visible aspect of circular action. They influence how companies, consumers, and policymakers view circularity.

5.6.4 Actor Triad: Businesses, Communities, Governments/Finance

Three actor groups surround the framework, connected with arrows pointing inward to show their roles as drivers and supporters:

- Businesses innovate and implement circular strategies.
- Communities provide resources (e.g., waste pickers, farmers) and gain benefits (jobs, income).
- Governments/Finance create a supportive environment through procurement, EPR policies, concessional finance, and regulation.

This triad recognizes that circular economy transitions involve multiple actors and require teamwork.

* Figure shows that circular transitions in developing economies involve several layers. Strategies need to be backed by operational capabilities, involve various actors, and be measured using CVP. Without this support, initiatives stay as isolated pilots. With it, they turn into scalable solutions for global sustainability challenges.

6 Future Research Directions

This element mainly focuses on how firms in developing economies are trying out circular economy (CE) practices by facing different challenges and by finding out the ways of getting support from communities, and governments. It provides insights into the EXIST Framework, it raises unresolved questions about theory, method, sector application, and systemic supports. Based on the insights from each section, this section suggests a research agenda to advance circular economy study and practice in developing contexts.

6.1 Theoretical Directions: Rethinking Circular Economy from the Global South

In the first section, we asked a simple but important question: how are businesses, communities, and governments in developing countries shaping the circular economy, and what challenges and chances do they meet on this path?

The case studies in this section begin to answer this question. However, most academic work on the circular economy still comes from the Global North. Key ideas in the field, from basic definitions (Kirchherr et al., 2017) to business models (Bocken et al., 2016) and broader frameworks (Geissdoerfer et al., 2017), are based on places with strong infrastructure, organized waste systems, and stable rules. These conditions are often missing in developing countries, where informality, limited public services, cultural practices, and uneven state capacity strongly influence how circular economy ideas are understood and used.

From our review (Table 9), three promising directions for future research stand out.

6.1.1 Rethinking the Circular Economy as Many Models, Not One

The circular economy is often described as one common model that can be used anywhere. In reality, it looks very different from place to place and

Table 9 Research gaps: rethinking circular economy from the global South

Gap identified	Example from cases	Future research direction
Global North-centric CE theory	Most typologies developed in Europe	Develop *"Southern Circularities"* that emphasize frugality, informality, and social embeddedness
Limited attention to socio-cultural factors	Phool's temple-waste valorization	Study how religion, culture, and traditions shape circular adoption
Under integration with development studies	ACT and Ecocitex rely on informal sector	Connect CE theory with inclusive innovation, livelihoods, and development policy

depends on local social, economic and political conditions (Schröder et al., 2020; Mukerjee et al., 2023). In many parts of the Global South, circular practices come from long standing habits of repair, reuse and careful use of resources. These are supported by informal systems that most mainstream ideas ignore, as they usually focus on advanced recycling technologies and large companies.

Examples such as Phool, All India Kabadiwala and the Trash Collectors Alliance (ACT) show that temple rituals and informal waste pickers play a central role in how circular practices actually work on the ground (Gutberlet, 2015; O'Hare et al., 2021). Future work on "Southern Circularities" (Schröder et al., 2020) can put justice, inclusion, informality and community relationships at the centre of circular thinking. This shifts us away from believing that a single model from the North can simply be copied in the South, and towards a deeper understanding of many different circular economies shaped by local histories, skills and social ties.

6.1.2 Connecting Sustainability Transitions with Development Studies

Most circular economy research looks at material flows, business models and industrial systems, often using ideas from ecological economics and industrial ecology (Babbitt et al., 2018). In doing so, it often overlooks deeper forces that shape change in developing economies, such as informal markets, weak institutions, long term inequality and limited state capacity. Work on sustainability transitions shows that change is rooted in local history and earlier decisions (Geels, 2002; Markard et al., 2012), but these insights are rarely used in circular economy research beyond European style settings.

Development studies offers a helpful contrast. It pays close attention to informality, inclusive innovation and deep rooted inequality (Pieterse, 2010; Heeks et al., 2014). Bringing this work together with circular economy research can show more clearly how circular practices emerge when money is tight or institutions are fragile, and how progress often depends on shared arrangements between informal workers, community groups and local governments. By combining these perspectives, we can move beyond simple images of closing the loop toward more grounded explanations of how circular practices start, grow or fade in complex contexts.

6.1.3 Paying Attention to Culture, Social Norms, and Everyday Behavior

Many studies show that culture and daily habits shape sustainability just as much as technology (Shove et al., 2012; Sahakian & Wilhite, 2014). Yet much circular economy writing still treats behaviour as individual, rational choice, instead of something shaped by shared norms.

The cases here show why culture matters. Phool works because it connects with the religious meaning of temple offerings. Ecocitex succeeds in part because Chile already has strong habits of reusing and repairing clothes. This supports other work showing that circular ideas spread more easily when they match local identities and stories (Corvellec et al., 2022). Overall, this points to a shift. The circular economy needs to be seen not only as a technical system, but also as a social and cultural process, especially in developing economies.

6.2 Methodological Directions: From Case Insights to Standardized Measurement

In this element, we used qualitative case-study methodology, which is good for exploration but limited in how widely its results can be applied. Future research needs to improve methodologies through:

6.2.1 CVP index development: A standard system for measuring impact is necessary. Future studies should improve CVP indicators, trial them across various sectors, and check their reliability. For example, comparing the CVP scores of Algramo (focused on reuse) and Attero (focused on recycling) could show how different strategies relate to impacts.

6.2.2 Mixed-methods research: Combining the depth of qualitative data with the breadth of quantitative data (such as case narratives and survey data) would balance exploration with generalization.

Please refer Table 10 for details regarding the gaps identified and the future research areas.

Table 10 Methodological research agenda

Methodological gap	Case relevance	Future research approach
Reliance on qualitative cases	11 startups studied	Scale up to **large-N surveys** and econometric validation
Lack of standardized CE metrics	Diverse reporting (jobs, waste diverted)	Develop and pilot **CVP index** with unified indicators

6.3 Empirical Directions: Expanding Sectors, Regions, and Scales

Section 4 analyzed diverse cases across sectors (flowers, agro-residues, plastics, e-waste, textiles) and geographies (Asia, Africa, Latin America). Building on this, future empirical research should:

6.3.1 Sectoral Deep Dives

Many research questions can be explored under this area such as Plastics and packaging: Study how refill and reuse models like Algramo can scale to mainstream?

FMCG. Textiles: Examine industrial-scale fiber-to-fiber recycling beyond upcycling (Ecocitex, ACT).

Agro-residues: Explore the potential of Craste and Cupffee's models to substitute conventional materials globally.

E-waste: Study how Attero's hybrid formal and informal approach can be replicated elsewhere.

6.3.2 Regional Comparisons

Compare how CE evolves in policy-rich settings (Chile, India) vs. informal-heavy contexts (Kenya, Nigeria).

6.3.3 Scaling Dynamics

Investigate tipping points that allow ventures to move from niche pilots to mainstream adoption. This includes factors like procurement contracts, EPR enforcement, or shifts in consumer behavior.

6.3.4 Equity Outcomes

Examine whether circular models fairly distribute benefits (e.g., women in Phool and informal workers in ACT) or risk reinforcing inequalities.

Please refer to Table 11 for details regarding the gaps identified and the future research areas.

6.4 Policy and Finance Directions: From Pilots to Systems

Policy and finance support for circular ventures is still uneven, but the examples in this study show that progress is possible. Attero has grown under early e-waste rules, Algramo has worked closely with city authorities, and ACT has relied on steady donor funding. These cases suggest that supportive conditions

Table 11 Empirical research opportunities

Sector/Region	Current case insights	Future research questions
Plastics/ Packaging	Algramo's refill systems	How can refill scale beyond niche adoption into FMCG mainstream?
Textiles	Ecocitex, ACT	Can fiber-to-fiber recycling become commercially viable at scale?
Agro-residues	Craste, Cupffee	How do bio-based boards/cups compete with synthetic substitutes?
E-waste	Attero	How can hybrid formal–informal recycling models be replicated regionally?
Regional	Chile vs. Kenya	Do strong policies accelerate CE scaling more than informal networks?

exist, yet they are not strong or stable enough to work at a larger scale. Future policies can focus on turning scattered pilot projects into reliable public systems, with cities acting as testing grounds through green purchasing, refund schemes for returned items and small incentives for bio based products. Extended Producer Responsibility also needs closer attention, especially in countries with limited capacity, where better enforcement methods such as community monitoring and digital tracking can improve results. New funding models that blend donor money, impact investment and bank finance, along with fair public private partnerships that balance business goals with social inclusion, will be essential.

6.5 Equity and Justice in Circular Economy

A common theme in this element is that circular economy in developing countries is closely linked to social equity.

Future research should:

- Study ways to formalize informal workers without harming their job security.
- Look into the gender aspects of circular work (e.g., women-led businesses like Phool).
- Examine the risks of exclusion if the circular economy becomes corporate and communities lose their waste-based jobs.
- Link circular economy research with the Just Transition framework to make sure climate action is fair for everyone.

7 Limitations

While this element significantly improves understanding of circular economy (CE) transitions in developing economies, several limitations must be acknowledged.

Case Scope and Selection – The analysis is based on eleven case studies across Asia, Africa, and Latin America. While diverse, these cases cannot capture the full variety of CE practices in all developing contexts. A selection bias toward innovative or well-known firms may also exclude informal or less-visible initiatives.

Sectoral Breadth vs. Depth – The cases cover multiple sectors, including e-waste, textiles, plastics, and agro-residues. However, each sector is represented by only one or two examples. There is a lack of deeper coverage in sectors like large-scale textile recycling ecosystems or municipal-level plastics loops.

Geographic Representation – Although covering three continents, the cases underrepresent regions such as the Middle East, Pacific Islands, or smaller African economies. Regional generalizations should thus be made with caution.

Methodological Boundaries – The book mainly uses qualitative, exploratory case analysis. While this method provides rich insights, it limits generalizability.

Data Reliability – Much of the impact data, such as waste diverted, jobs created, and CO_2 avoided, was self-reported by companies. Independent, audited data would strengthen reliability.

Dynamic Transitions – Circular transitions are dynamic and evolve as policies, technologies, and markets change. The book provides a snapshot in time, so findings may require revision as contexts evolve.

8 Implications

8.1 Policy Implications

The findings of this element indicate that transitions to a circular economy in developing countries cannot rely solely on entrepreneurial innovation. Without supportive policy and governance systems, successful projects will remain scattered.

Green Public Procurement (GPP): Governments should commit to buying goods made from recycled or bio-based materials. For example, agro-boards (Craste), recycled textiles (Ecocitex), and edible cups (Cupffee) can be used in municipal supply chains. This type of procurement creates reliable markets and reduces risk for innovators.

Extended Producer Responsibility (EPR): Attero's success in e-waste recycling shows the potential of EPR. However, enforcement is weak in most sectors. Governments should broaden EPR to cover plastics, textiles, and packaging, supported by monitoring tools like blockchain traceability.

Financing Mechanisms: Circular start-ups often struggle with financing gaps known as the "valley of death." Blended finance models that combine concessional capital, guarantees, and impact investment can reduce investment risks. Governments and multilateral agencies could create Circular Economy Funds to help businesses grow.

Inclusion of Informal Sector: Waste pickers and community recyclers (e.g., ACT, Ecocitex) are key players in the circular economy in the Global South. Policies should support their formalization without pushing them out of their roles, using cooperatives, certifications, and social protections.

Education and Capacity Building: To achieve lasting change, circular economy concepts should be included in school curricula, municipal training programs, and public awareness efforts.

8.2 Managerial and Entrepreneurial Implications

The cases in this element are not just inspiring stories. They offer practical lessons for entrepreneurs, managers and ecosystem builders who want to shape their own circular economy efforts. They show that circular models work not only because they close the loop, but because they focus on relationships, resource flows and community ties.

One clear lesson is the need for reliable sources of materials. Circular businesses depend on steady access to waste or byproducts. Attero built long term agreements with municipalities for e-waste and plastics. Phool partnered with temples to collect flowers at scale. Craste and Releaf worked with farmer groups to turn crop residues into useful inputs. These examples show that supply in circular systems is built on trust, shared values and close work with local communities. Another insight is that using more than one circular strategy makes firms stronger. Attero combines Close and Enable strategies. Algramo blends Slow and Enable. Phool uses parts of Regenerate and Narrow. This mix helps companies grow, spread risk and adapt to changing customers and policies.

The cases also show how social and commercial goals can go together. Firms like Phool, Ecocitex and ACT earn revenue while supporting social inclusion and better livelihoods. The most successful ones can clearly measure and explain their impact, which matters to investors. This makes good impact measurement essential. Tools such as CVP help firms show their environmental, social and economic results in a clear way, guide decisions and build trust.

Finally, circular business is about shaping ecosystems, not just single firms. The most durable solutions come from entrepreneurs who work with governments, civil society, informal workers, suppliers and consumers. Circularity, especially in the Global South, grows through shared effort.

Abbreviation Full Form

ACES	Aces Global Innovation Challenge (UNC)
ACT	Africa Collect Textiles
ADB	Asian Development Bank
AI	Artificial Intelligence
B2B	Business-to-Business
B2C	Business-to-Consumer
CE	Circular Economy
CSR	Corporate Social Responsibility
GDP	Gross Domestic Product
ICT	Information and Communication Technology
IIT	Indian Institute of Technology
IoT	Internet of Things
IT	Information Technology
NGO	Non-Governmental Organization
R&D	Research and Development
SD	Sustainable Development
SDGs	Sustainable Development Goals
SMEs	Small and Medium Enterprises
UN	United Nations
UNEP	United Nations Environment Programme
UNESCO	United Nations Educational, Scientific and Cultural Organization
UNFCCC	United Nations Framework Convention on Climate Change
USA	United States of America
UK	United Kingdom
WB	World Bank
WTO	World Trade Organization

References

Adams, H. (2021, June 3). *Agritech startup, Fortuna's, plastic-free coconut coolers. Food and Drink Digital*. Retrieved March 7, 2026, from https://l1nq.com/gx1o6h7.

Africa Collect Textiles. (2025, May 20). *Closing the loop: How Africa Collect Textiles is tackling fashion waste. AMI Plastics*. Retrieved August 23, 2025, from https://sl1nk.com/wlqqat5.

Africa Collect Textiles. (n.d.). *Home*. Retrieved August 14, 2025, from https://africacollecttextiles.com/.

Africa News. (2022, October 23). *Kenya struggles to recycle growing volumes of textile waste*. Retrieved March 7, 2026, from https://l1nq.com/6msctzt.

Africanews. (2021, November 2). *Kenya: Africa Collect Textiles collects and recycles used clothes*. Retrieved March 7, 2026, from https://sl1nk.com/er9c5nv.

Aggeri, F. (2021). From waste to urban mines: A historical perspective on the circular economy. *Field Actions Science Reports*, Special Issue 23, 10–13. https://journals.openedition.org/factsreports/6530.

Ajiboye, K. (2025, March 21). *Salubata: Redefining footwear with style and comfort. Independent Newspaper Nigeria*. Retrieved March 7, 2026, from https://sl1nk.com/gzp1mcx.

Akinse, F. (2022, June 25). *Salubata: Recycling plastics to footwear. The Guardian Nigeria*. Retrieved March 7, 2026, from https://l1nq.com/lt5fbjo.

Ambani, S. (2021, February 27). *Engineer turning plastic waste into paving bricks. Daily Nation*. Retrieved March 7, 2026, from https://sl1nk.com/a43e5k8.

AMI Plastics. (2023). *How Africa Collect Textiles is tackling fashion waste*. Retrieved March 7, 2026, from https://sl1nk.com/1zdk1i0.

Architectural Technology. (2021, February 15). *Kenyan start-up recycles plastic bottles into bricks stronger than concrete*. Retrieved March 7, 2026, from https://l1nq.com/o5ynxas.

Arenas, V. (2022, November 21). *El difícil negocio de reciclar la ropa usada*. Forbes Chile. Retrieved August 14, 2025, from https://sl1nk.com/agkktec.

Arthavaan. (2021). Phool: Social entrepreneurship and circular economy. *Arthavaan Journal*, *1*(1), 49–54. Retrieved March 7, 2026, from https://www.arthavaan.org/files/IssueContent/D–11.pdf.

Arthavaan. (2022). Craste: Turning crop waste into a sustainable future. Retrieved March 7, 2026, from https://missionsustainability.org/blog/craste/.

Asharq Al Awsat. (2021, February 2). Kenyan recycles plastic waste into bricks stronger than concrete. Retrieved March 7, 2026, from https://sl1nk.com/i0d63vm.

Atlas of the Future. (2022). Gjenge makers. Retrieved March 7, 2026, from https://atlasofthefuture.org/project/gjenge-makers/.

Attero Recycling Pvt. Ltd. (n.d.). *Attero Recycling Pvt. Ltd.* Environmental-Expert. Retrieved August 10, 2025, from https://l1nq.com/6kuayku.

Babbitt, C. W., Gaustad, G., Fisher, A., Chen, W., & Liu, G. (2018). Closing the loop on circular economy research: From theory to practice. *Resources, Conservation and Recycling, 135*, 1–2. https://doi.org/10.1016/j.resconrec.2018.03.017.

Bakker, C. A., den Hollander, M. C., Van Hinte, E., & Klaassen, R. (2014). *Products that last: Product design for circular business models*. TU Delft.

Bate, C. (2022, July 20). Bühler, Cupffee up edible coffee cup production. *PKN Packaging News*. Retrieved March 7, 2026, from https://sl1nk.com/a5560yl.

BBM Magazine. (2022, July 20). Reducing plastic waste with edible coffee cups. Retrieved March 7, 2026, from https://sl1nk.com/uinwjip.

Berkes, F. (2008). *Sacred ecology* (2nd ed.). Routledge. https://doi.org/10.4324/9780203928950.

Bharat Economic Forum. (2022, July 18). Phool.co: A social enterprise turning flower waste into opportunity. Retrieved March 7, 2026, from https://l1nq.com/dpyhpu9.

Bocken, N. M. P., Bakker, C., & Pauw, I. (2016). Product design and business model strategies for a circular economy. *Journal of Industrial and Production Engineering, 33*(5), 308–320. https://doi.org/10.1080/21681015.2016.1142129.

Bocken, N. M. P., de Pauw, I., Bakker, C., & van der Grinten, B. (2016). Product life extension and business models: Exploring the case of lighting. *Journal of Industrial and Production Engineering, 33*(5), 308–320. https://doi.org/10.1080/21681015.2016.1142129.

Bocken, N. M. P., de Pauw, I., Bakker, C., & van der Grinten, B. (2019). Product design and business model strategies for a circular economy. *Journal of Industrial and Production Engineering, 36*(5), 273–278. https://doi.org/10.1080/21681015.2019.1578090.

Bocken, N. M. P., Tukker, A., & Bakker, C. (2016). Product design and business models for a circular economy. In A. Charteris (Ed.), *Handbook of sustainable design* (pp. 165–181). Edward Elgar Publishing.

Brandenburg, M. (2015). Supply chain management in the circular economy: A literature review. *Logistics Research, 8*(1), 1–13. https://doi.org/10.1007/s12159-015-0125-8.

Cairns, R. (2021, October 29). This Philippines startup is making coolers out of coconuts. *CNN*. Retrieved March 7, 2026, from https://sl1nk.com/5t96rzo.

Caldow, D. (2025). Powering change through partnerships and collaboration. *Ellen MacArthur Foundation*. Retrieved March 7, 2026, from https://sl1nk.com/4fuhvw5.

CanvasBusinessModel.com. (2024, October 2). A brief history of Phool. Retrieved August 1, 2025, from https://l1nq.com/3n02ygn.

Causeartist. (2020). The modern sustainable cooler made from coconut waste. Retrieved March 7, 2026, from https://sl1nk.com/buk3zhm.

Causeartist. (2021, April 19). Nutshell coolers are replacing plastic foam with coconut fiber insulation. Retrieved March 7, 2026, from https://l1nq.com/ojsypym.

Chowdhary, S. (2020, September 12). Phool.co: Solving the temple waste problem. *The Financial Express*. Retrieved March 7, 2026, from https://l1nq.com/3t5u8wb.

Closed Loop Partners. (2020a, July 22). Closed loop partners' center for the circular economy launches reuse pilot with Algramo in New York city. Retrieved March 7, 2026, from https://sl1nk.com/oxpyd5d.

Closed Loop Partners. (2020b, October 14). Closed loop partners invests in Algramo to advance affordable, reusable packaging systems. Retrieved March 7, 2026, from https://sl1nk.com/zdlhndu.

Contxto. (2020, July 2). *Chilean sustainability startup Algramo competes in Ocean Plastic Innovation Challenge*. Retrieved March 7, 2026, from https://l1nq.com/6m6qpx2.

Coombe, S. (2023, March 9). *Spinning a sustainable yarn: Zero waste textiles in Chile. Resource Magazine*. Retrieved March 7, 2026, from https://l1nq.com/wr6q64s.

Cooper, T. (2005). Slower consumption: Reflections on product life spans and the "throwaway society." *Journal of Industrial Ecology*, *9*(1–2), 51–67. https://doi.org/10.1162/1088198054084671.

Corvellec, H., Stål, H. I., & Lindhqvist, T. (2022). Critiques of the circular economy. *Journal of Industrial Ecology*, *26*(2), 484–497. https://doi.org/10.1111/jiec.13100.

Craste. (n.d.). *Craste – We build it better*. Retrieved August 12, 2025, from https://craste.co/.

Cupffee. (n.d.). *About us*. https://www.cupffee.me/en/about-us.

Danov, R. (2023, January 11). Ukrainian startup Releaf Paper raises €2.5 million from the European Commission. *Releaf Paper*. https://l1nq.com/dho13l2.

Diario Sustentable. (2021, October 12). *Algramo recognized by Fortune magazine as one of the 20 startups with the greatest social and environmental impact globally*. Retrieved March 7, 2026, from https://l1nq.com/vwl8me2.

Diario Sustentable. (2022, September 12). *Algramo named the most innovative reuse company globally*. Retrieved March 7, 2026, from https://sl1nk.com/9o9ty7f.

Ecocitex. (n.d.). *Inicio*. Retrieved August 14, 2025, from https://www.ecocitex.cl/.

Economic Times. (2024, June 28). *Attero launches e-waste recycling platform "Selsmart" for consumers*. Retrieved March 7, 2026, from https://sl1nk.com/5sho7qu.

Eisenhardt, K. M. (1989). Building theories from case study research. *Academy of Management Review, 14*(4), 532–550. https://doi.org/10.5465/amr.1989.4308385.

Ellen MacArthur Foundation. (2013). *Towards the circular economy, Vol. 1: An economic and business rationale for an industry transition*. www.ellenmacarthurfoundation.org.

Ellen MacArthur Foundation. (2015). *Growth within: A circular economy story*. www.ellenmacarthurfoundation.org.

Ellen MacArthur Foundation. (2015). *Towards a circular economy: Business rationale for an accelerated transition*. www.ellenmacarthurfoundation.org.

Elsässer, M. (2025, September 5). *Releaf paper: Eco packaging from leaves disrupts paper. StartupValley*. Retrieved March 7, 2026, from https://startupvalley.news/uk/releaf-paper-eco-packaging/.

En-SJGLE. (2021). *Startup turns coconut husks into sustainable coolers*. Retrieved March 7, 2026, from www.en-sjgle.com/news/show-22296.html.

Escapethecity.org. (n.d.). *Algramo profile*. Retrieved March 7, 2026, from www.escapethecity.org/organisation/algramo.

Euronews. (2023, September 25). *Meet the Kenyan woman turning plastics into bricks*. Retrieved March 7, 2026, from https://l1nq.com/qwzxjwb.

European Commission. (2015a). *Closing the loop – An EU action plan for the circular economy* (COM/2015/0614 final). Publications Office of the European Union.

European Commission. (2015b). *Communication from the commission to the European parliament, the council, the European economic and social committee and the committee of the regions: Closing the loop – An EU action plan for the circular economy*. https://eur-lex.europa.eu/legal-content/EN/TXT/?uri=CELEX:52015DC0614.

European Commission. (2019). *Report on the implementation of the Circular Economy Action Plan*. Retrieved March 7, 2026, from https://sl1nk.com/uhievca.

Financial Express. (2020, September 19). *Blockchain: Phool.co – Solving the temple waste problem*. Retrieved March 7, 2026, from https://sl1nk.com/objd5su.

Food and Drink Digital. (2021, September 27). *Fortuna Cools: Agritech startup makes plastic-free coconut coolers*. Retrieved March 7, 2026, from https://www.fooddigital.com.

Fortuna Cools. (n.d.). *Our story*. Retrieved August 13, 2025, from www.fortunacools.com.

Fremong, A. (2022, February 3). *The sole of a Nigerian entrepreneur*. ACES – Ackerman Center for Excellence in Sustainability. Retrieved March 7, 2026, from https://l1nq.com/9vlg80x.

Frenken, K., & Schor, J. (2017). Putting the sharing economy into perspective. *Environmental Innovation and Societal Transitions*, *23*, 3–10. https://doi.org/10.1016/j.eist.2017.01.003.

Global Center on Adaptation. (2021). *African Youth Adaptation Solutions Challenge (YouthADAPT) – Cycle 1*. https://l1nq.com/0d9bmxn.

Geels, F. W. (2002). Technological transitions as evolutionary reconfiguration processes. *Research Policy*, *31*(8–9), 1257–1274. https://doi.org/10.1016/S0048-7333(02)00062-8.

Geissdoerfer, M., Savaget, P., Bocken, N. M. P., & Hultink, E. J. (2017). The circular economy: A new sustainability paradigm? *Journal of Cleaner Production*, *143*, 757–768. https://doi.org/10.1016/j.jclepro.2016.12.048.

Geyer, R. (n.d.). *Reuse & recycling*. Retrieved August 14, 2025, from www.rolandgeyer.com/.

Geyer, R. (2020). Production, use, and fate of synthetic polymers. *Nature Reviews Materials*, *5*, 391–408. 10.1016/B978-0-12-817880-5.00002-5.

Ghisellini, P., Cialani, C., & Ulgiati, S. (2016a). A review on circular economy: The expected transition to a balanced interplay of environmental and economic systems. *Journal of Cleaner Production*, *114*, 11–32. https://doi.org/10.1016/j.jclepro.2015.09.088.

Ghisellini, P., Cialani, C., & Ulgiati, S. (2016b). From "linear" to "circular" economy: A review of micro-level input–output studies. *Journal of Cleaner Production*, *114*, 51–65. https://doi.org/10.1016/j.jclepro.2015.09.088.

Glaser, B., & Strauss, A. (1967). *Discovery of grounded theory: Strategies for qualitative research*. Routledge.

Global Center on Adaptation. (2021, November 8). *YouthADAPT Challenge: Salubata*. Retrieved March 7, 2026, from https://gca.org/youthadapt/salubata/.

Goyal, S., & Sergi, B. S. (2020). *Towards a theory of "smart" social infrastructures at base of the pyramid: A study of India*. Cambridge University Press.

Green Queen. (2021, October 14). *Fortuna Cools secures seed round to replace Styrofoam with coconut coolers*. Retrieved March 7, 2026, from www.greenqueen.com.hk.

Guardian Nigeria. (2024, October 25). *Addressing climate challenges: The impact of Salubata and the NBA Africa triple-double accelerator*. Retrieved March 7, 2026, from https://l1nq.com/0wnqrom.

Gupta, N. (2012). Nitin Gupta of Attero on what it takes to build a global cleantech business from India. *YourStory*. Retrieved March 7, 2026, from https://sl1nk.com/nel1meq.

Gutberlet, J. (2012). Informal and cooperative recycling as a poverty alleviation strategy. *Geography Compass*, *9*(9), 391–408. https://doi.org/10.1111/j.1749-8198.2012.00512.x.

Gutberlet, J. (2015). More inclusive and cleaner cities with waste management co-production: Insights from participatory epistemologies and practices. *Habitat International*, *46*, 234–243. https://doi.org/10.1016/j.habitatint.2014.10.004.

Gómez, F. (2023, April 14). *Ecocitex: La empresa chilena que busca reciclar 20 toneladas de ropa al año*. Pauta. Retrieved March 7, 2026, from https://l1nq.com/nyjo508.

Heeks, R., Foster, C., & Nugroho, Y. (2014). New models of inclusive innovation for development. *Innovation and Development*, *4*(2), 175–185. https://doi.org/10.1080/2157930X.2014.928982.

HighPerformr.ai. (n.d.). *Algramo company profile*. Retrieved March 7, 2026, from www.highperformr.ai/company/algramo.

Pereira, R., Ferreira, E. A., Alves, J. L., de Nadae, J., & Galvão, G. D. A. (2020). Circular economy and supply chain: A scientific characterization. *Brazilian Journal of Operations & Production Management*, *17*(4), 1–17. https://doi.org/10.14488/BJOPM.2020.048.

Houser, K. (2021, February 11). *DIY factory turns plastic waste into super-strong bricks*. Freethink. Retrieved March 7, 2026, from www.freethink.com/energy/bricks-made-from-plastic-waste.

Ihekire, C. (2021, March 20). *Salubata ... recycling plastics to footwear. Guardian Nigeria*. Retrieved March 7, 2026, from https://guardian.ng/saturday-magazine/salubata-recycling-plastics-to-footwear/.

IIT Kanpur. (2022). *Phool.co selected as Earthshot Prize finalist.* Retrieved March 7, 2026, from https://vifindia.org + https://iitk.ac.in + www.hindustantimes.com.

IMPACC. (n.d.). *Gjenge Makers is building material from plastic waste* [Start-up profile]. IMPACC – Start-Up Africa. Retrieved March 7, 2026, from www.impacc.org/en/venture/gjenge-makers/.

India Today. (2023, July 26). *From trash to treasure: The how and why of segregating waste.* Retrieved March 7, 2026, from www.indiatoday.in/information/story/from-trash-to-treasure-the-how-and-why-of-segregating-waste-2411957-2023-07-26.

India Today. (2025, February 4). *Introduce incentives for e-waste recycling, experts suggest to boost participation.* Retrieved March 7, 2026, from https://sl1nk.com/e3mwm3q.

Indian Express. (2024, February 20). *Stubble burning sowed the seeds of this startup. The Indian Express.* Retrieved March 7, 2026, from https://l1nq.com/z87kte7.

Ingredients Network. (2021, October 1). *Fortuna Cools raises funding to launch coconut-based sustainable cooler boxes.* Retrieved March 7, 2026, from www.ingredientsnetwork.com.

Katanich, D. (2020, December 16). *Kenyan women turn plastic waste into bricks stronger than concrete* [Video]. *Euronews.* Retrieved March 7, 2026, from https://l1nq.com/dea7i0z.

Kaza, S., Yao, L. C., Bhada-Tata, P., & Van Woerden, F. (2018, September 20). *What a waste 2.0: A global snapshot of solid waste management to 2050. World Bank.* Retrieved October 7, 2025, from https://datatopics.worldbank.org/what-a-waste/.

KEEN Effect. (2021, March 10). *How Gjenge Makers is turning plastic waste into building materials.* Retrieved March 7, 2026, from www.keenfootwear.com/keen.effect/blog-article-210310.html.

Kirchherr, J., Reike, D., & Hekkert, M. (2017). Conceptualizing the circular economy: An analysis of 114 definitions. *Resources, Conservation and Recycling, 127*, 221–232. https://doi.org/10.1016/j.resconrec.2017.09.005.

Korhonen, J., Honkasalo, A., & Seppälä, J. (2018). Circular economy: The concept and its limitations. *Ecological Economics, 143*, 37–46. https://doi.org/10.1016/j.ecolecon.2017.06.041.

Kostadinova, R. (2023, May 23). *Bulgarian Cupffee secures €1.8M with its edible coffee cups. Trending Topics.* Retrieved March 7, 2026, from www.trendingtopics.eu/bulgarian-cupffee-secures-e1-8m-with-its-edible-coffee-cups/.

Lecumberri, B. (2024, November 27). *Why putting used clothes in a recycling bin does not allow you to have a clear conscience. EL PAÍS*. Retrieved March 7, 2026, from https://sl1nk.com/du1hd2f.

Lieder, M., & Rashid, A. (2016). Towards circular economy implementation: A comprehensive review in context of manufacturing industry. *Journal of cleaner production*, *115*, 36–51. https://doi.org/10.1016/j.jclepro.2015.12.042.

Maier, J., Geyer, R., & Zink, T. (2020). Circular economy rebound. In M. Brandão, D. Lazarevic, & G. Finnveden (Eds.), *Handbook of the circular economy* (pp. 194–205). Edward Elgar Publishing.

Marico Innovation Foundation. (2023). *Solving India's crop waste conundrum with Craste's innovative farmer-first technology*. Retrieved March 7, 2026, from https://l1nq.com/ctw6yie.

Markard, J., Raven, R., & Truffer, B. (2012). Sustainability transitions: An emerging field of research and its prospects. *Research Policy*, *41*(6), 955–967. https://doi.org/10.1016/j.respol.2012.02.013.

Matthis, S. (2024, December 16). *Startup company Releaf Paper begins producing pulp from fallen leaves. PULPAPERnews*. Retrieved March 7, 2026, from https://sl1nk.com/hwqtfa9.

McCabe, S. (2021, Spring). *Unbreakable bricks: Transforming plastic waste. SWE Magazine*. Retrieved March 7, 2026.

Meadows, D. H. (2008). *Thinking in systems: A primer*. Chelsea Green Publishing.

Mekler, T. (2024). *The Internet's coolest cooler: Coconut husks as hero insulation. The Resilience Report*. Retrieved November 7, 2025, from https://l1nq.com/rdflht4.

Michail, N. (2020, March 26). *Sustainable start-up Algramo sells Nestlé, Unilever products in reusable packaging. FoodNavigator Latam*. Retrieved March 7, 2026, from https://sl1nk.com/ok5309x.

Miles, M. B. (1979). Qualitative data as an attractive nuisance: The problem of analysis. *Administrative Science Quarterly*, *24*(4), 590–615. https://doi.org/10.2307/2392365.

Miliani, A. (2022, April 21). Inside a Chilean factory turning old clothes into high quality eco yarn. *Vogue*. Retrieved March 7, 2026, from www.vogue.com/article/inside-ecocitex-yarn-factory.

Musmanni, G. D. (2023, April 21). How one Nigerian enterprise is tackling the global plastic plague, one shoe at a time. *Global Center on Adaptation*. Retrieved March 7, 2026, from https://sl1nk.com/bw7vfsw.

Nabi, S. (2025, May 13). *The sacred cycle: How a company in Kanpur is giving India's flower waste a second life. The Conversationalist*. Retrieved March 7, 2026, from https://sl1nk.com/o52lz7s.

Nation Africa. (2024, March 28). *Entrepreneur finds success turning textile waste into carpets and padding for sofas, toys*. https://sl1nk.com/xhbfljn.

Nation Media Group. (2021, February 25). *Engineer turning plastic waste into paving bricks. Daily Nation*. https://l1nq.com/jauq0y8.

Ndambuki, S. (2024, July 11). *Entrepreneur finds success turning textile waste into carpets and padding for sofas, toys. Daily Nation*. Retrieved March 7, 2026, from https://l1nq.com/cx65aib.

Neira, J. (2021, February 8). *Gjenge Makers recycles plastic into bricks stronger than concrete. DesignBoom*. Retrieved March 7, 2026, from https://l1nq.com/1k7bw94.

NESsT. (n.d.). *Ecocitex*. Retrieved March 7, 2026, from www.nesst.org/ecocitex.

OECD. (2022, April). *Global plastics outlook: Economic drivers, environmental impacts and policy options*. Retrieved March 7, 2026, from https://sl1nk.com/3fnp5qr.

Omondi, P. (2022, March 12). *Building a better future with recycled plastic. WIPO Magazine*. Retrieved March 7, 2026, from https://l1nq.com/p9i3mkt.

Our Better World. (2021, June 24). *Dirty to dignified: These flowers transform lives*. Retrieved March 7, 2026, from https://l1nq.com/dbqhorx.

Outlook Business. (2021, December 17). *On the banks of the Ganges, blooms a start-up called Phool*. Retrieved March 7, 2026, from https://sl1nk.com/tvfkiaa.

Pearce, D. W., & Turner, R. K. (1990). *Economics of natural resources and the environment*. Johns Hopkins University Press.

Peters, A. (2019, October 14). *This startup is ditching plastic waste by bringing the refills to you. Fast Company*. Retrieved March 7, 2026, from https://l1nq.com/adj0rta.

Peters, A. (2020, August 25). *This cleaning product refill service will help New York consumers ditch single-use plastic. Fast Company*. Retrieved March 7, 2026, from https://sl1nk.com/rhopxli.

Pieterse, J. N. (2010). *Development theory: Deconstructions/reconstructions* (2nd ed.). Sage Publications.

Platform for Accelerating the Circular Economy (PACE). (2020). *What is a circular economy?* World Economic Forum & World Resources Institute. Retrieved March 7, 2026, from https://pacecircular.org/about.

Plank, M., & Bocken, N. (2017). Design for circular business models: A review. *Journal of Cleaner Production*, *159*, 137–151. https://doi.org/10.1016/j.jclepro.2017.04.148.

PM News Nigeria. (2022, June 22). *Nigeria's Salubata tech wins $10,000 prize at kigali start-up festival*. Retrieved November 7, 2026, from https://l1nq.com/0f0fnoi.

Ponting, C. (2007). *A new green history of the world: The environment and the collapse of great civilizations*. Penguin Books.

Preethi, M. (2025, June 16). This cleantech company recycles your phones, batteries to extract precious metals & reduce e-waste. *The Better India*. Retrieved March 7, 2026, from https://sl1nk.com/7lf4dqh.

Preqin. (n.d.). *Fortuna cools* [company profile]. Retrieved March 7, 2026, from https://sl1nk.com/2re1psr.

Preston, F. (2012). *A global redesign? Shaping the circular economy*. Chatham House.

Publimetro. (2020, September 24). *Microsoft supports the growth of Algramo through its startup program* [Original work published in Spanish]. Retrieved March 7, 2026, from https://l1nq.com/tjh35m9.

Radio France Internationale. (2025, May 3). *The Kenyan engineer building a sustainable future with recycled plastic bricks*. Retrieved March 7, 2026, from https://sl1nk.com/n978s7n.

Ramadurai, C. (2023, February 17). *Where have all the flowers gone? India starts recycling religious ceremony leftovers*. *The National*. Retrieved March 7, 2026, from www.thenationalnews.com.

Reddit. (2025). *Startup idea: Think Uber/Swiggy for scrap dealers – app for buying/selling e-waste*. Retrieved March 7, 2026, from www.reddit.com/r/Startup_Ideas/comments/1imrv62.

Reike, D., Vermeulen, W. J., & Witjes, S. (2018). The circular economy: New or refurbished as CE 3.0? – exploring controversies in the conceptualization of the circular economy through a focus on history and resource value retention options. *Resources, conservation and recycling*, *135*, 246-264. https://doi.org/10.1016/j.resconrec.2017.08.027.

Releaf Paper. (2022, June 20). *This energy-efficient technology turns fallen leaves into paper*. Retrieved March 7, 2026, from https://l1nq.com/n11l63s.

Releaf Paper. (2023a). *News and updates*. Retrieved March 7, 2026, from www.releaf-paper.com/news.

Releaf Paper. (2023b, September 12). *Releaf Paper opens pilot production line in France*. Retrieved March 7, 2026, from https://l1nq.com/1gkj9lq.

Releaf Paper. (n.d.). *Releaf Paper – Manufacturer of paper made from fallen leaves*. Retrieved March 7, 2026, from www.releaf-paper.com/.

Rembre. (2024, February 27). *El reciclaje textil: El nuevo desafío de Rembre. Diario Financiero*. Retrieved March 7, 2026, from https://l1nq.com/0qzb6tj.

Resource. (2022, November 15). *Spinning sustainable yarn: Zero-waste textiles in Chile*. Retrieved March 7, 2026, from https://sl1nk.com/zm6c2gs.

Schröder, P., & MacEwen, M. (2021, June 17). *What is the circular economy?* Chatham House. Retrieved March 7, 2026, from www.chathamhouse.org/2021/06/what-circular-economy.

Schröder, P., Lemille, A., & Desmond, P. (2020). Making the circular economy work for human development. *Circular Economy and Sustainability*, *1*(1), 307–328.

Shove, E., Pantzar, M., & Watson, M. (2012). *The dynamics of social practice*. Sage.

Sinha, M. (2025, January 1). On the banks of the Ganges, blooms a start-up called Phool. *Outlook Business*. Retrieved March 7, 2026, from https://l1nq.com/y4pu2az.

Sobachynskyi, R. (2023, May 23). Bulgarian company Cupffee raises €1.8M for its edible coffee cups. *AIN.UA*. Retrieved March 7, 2026, from https://l1nq.com/00e0rkc.

Society of Women Engineers. (2021). *Unbreakable bricks: Transforming plastic waste*. Retrieved March 7, 2026, from https://sl1nk.com/dl7e8e5.

Southey, F. (2023, May 31). Cupffee: Edible coffee cup developed from oat bran and wheat flour. *FoodNavigator*. Retrieved November 19, 2025, from https://sl1nk.com/95jabnh.

Stahel, W. R. (1982). The product-life factor. In *An inquiry into the nature of sustainable societies: The role of the private sector*. Mitchell Prize Foundation.

Stahel, W. R. (2010). *The performance economy* (2nd ed.). Palgrave Macmillan.

Stahel, W. R. (2016). The circular economy. *Nature*, 531(7595), 435. https://doi.org/10.1038/531435a.

Stahel, W. R. (2019). *The circular economy: A user's guide*. Routledge.

Stahel, W. R., & Reday-Mulvey, G. (1976). The potential for substituting manpower for energy. Report to the European Commission.

StartUpTalky. (2023, August 21). *Phool – Turning flower waste into incense sticks and sustainable products*. Retrieved November 19, 2025, from https://startuptalky.com/phool-success-story/.

Suneja, K. (2013, January 21). E-waste everywhere, not enough to treat. *Business Standard*. Retrieved November 19, 2025, from https://l1nq.com/swrxo9n.

Sustainable Brands. (2020a, July 23). *Algramo expands reusable packaging platform to New York City*. https://l1nq.com/69av0q1.

Sustainable Brands. (2020b, October 21). *Algramo brings refillable, waste-free cleaning products to NYC*. https://l1nq.com/dnfmyzt.

Swahili Design Lab. (2023). *How plastic bricks are revolutionizing Kenya's environmental landscape*. https://l1nq.com/exqdy10.

The Star. (2023, April 10). How textile upcycling firm is reaping from circular economy. https://sl1nk.com/qgaxd1b.

The Startup Lab. (2021, August 4). Craste is creating value-added products out of crop residue for furniture and packaging applications. https://l1nq.com/3j12366.

The StoryWatch. (2023). This company is solving two major problems – plastic packaging and stubble burning – with their innovative technology. https://l1nq.com/izgrlw0.

ThePrint. (2023). *How flowercycling and Fleather were born*. IIT Kanpur. https://theprint.in/.

Thompson, M. (1979). *Rubbish theory: The creation and destruction of value*. Oxford University Press.

Times of India. (2021, March 4). Company backed by IIT-K wins award for bioalternative to animal leather. https://l1nq.com/dm2cq3w.

Times of India. (2025, March 17). India's e-waste time bomb: As volumes surge, gaps in recycling widen. https://l1nq.com/8ou7gae.

Times of India. (2021, March 4). Company backed by IIT-K wins award for bioalternative to animal leather. https://sl1nk.com/8iyoyke.

Times of India. (2025, March 17). India's e-waste time bomb: As volumes surge, gaps in recycling widen. https://sl1nk.com/t32gdsv.

Trahant, G. (2021, July 28). The Nutshell sustainable cooler is leading the transition from plastic foam to natural fiber packaging. *Causeartist*. Retrieved March 7, 2026, from www.causeartist.com/modern-sustainable-cooler-nutshell/.

Tukker, A. (2015a). Product services for a resource-efficient and circular economy: A review. *Journal of Cleaner Production*, *97*, 76–91. https://doi.org/10.1016/j.jclepro.2013.11.049.

Tukker, A. (2015b). Product–service systems: From products to services in a circular economy. *Journal of Cleaner Production*, *97*, 1–13.

Tuko.co.ke. (2021). Nzambi Matee: Gjenge Makers founder speaks on her award-winning trash-to-cash innovation. Retrieved March 7, 2026, from https://sl1nk.com/h85wvz0.

Tuladhar, A., Iatridis, K., & Dimov, D. (2021). History and evolution of the circular economy and circular economy business models. In A. Stefanakis & I. Nikolaou (Eds.), *Circular economy and sustainability: Environmental engineering, policy, and management* (pp. 187–192). Elsevier. https://doi.org/10.1016/B978-0-12-819817-9.00031-4.

United Nations Environment Programme. (2020). *Young champions of the Earth: Nzambi Matee*. Retrieved March 7, 2026, from https://sl1nk.com/dqf42qb.

United Nations Environment Programme. (2023). *José Manuel Moller: Champions of the earth*. Retrieved March 7, 2026, from https://sl1nk.com/ohm5z30.

United Nations Environment Programme. (2023c, September 21). *Chilean start-up changing our relationship with plastic*. Retrieved March 7, 2026, from https://sl1nk.com/h6itaqi.

United Nations Environment Programme. (2024). *Global waste management outlook 2024*. Retrieved March 7, 2026, from https://sl1nk.com/gdshm4w.

United Nations Educational, Scientific and Cultural Organization. (2021). Phool: A story of change. Retrieved March 7, 2026, from www.unesco.org/en/articles/phool-story-change.

University of North Carolina at Chapel Hill. (2022). *Salubata: Modular shoes from recycled plastic waste*. UNC ACES Global Innovation Challenge. Retrieved November 15, 2025, from https://aces.unc.edu/salubata.

United Nations Environment Programme (UNEP). (2018). *Africa waste management outlook*. Retrieved March 7, 2026, from https://wedocs.unep.org/20.500.11822/25514.

United Nations Framework Convention on Climate Change (UNFCCC). (2023). *Phool | India*. Retrieved March 7, 2026, from https://l1nq.com/7ft87ly.

UNC Kenan Institute. (2022). *The sole of a Nigerian entrepreneur*. Retrieved March 7, 2026, from https://sl1nk.com/6h2xvup.

Vellum Kenya. (2024, February 14). Towards zero waste: How East Africa is handling the textile waste crisis. Retrieved March 7, 2026, from https://l1nq.com/caxmjuv.

Vezzoli, C., Ceschin, F., Diehl, J. C., & Kohtala, C. (2015). New design challenges to widely implement sustainable product–service systems. *Journal of Cleaner Production*, *97*, 1–12. https://doi.org/10.1016/j.jclepro.2014.01.039.

Vezzoli, C., & Manzini, E. (2008). *Design for environmental sustainability*. Springer. https://doi.org/10.1007/978-1-84800-163-3.

WA Contents. (2021, February 12). Kenyan startup founder Nzambi Matee recycles plastic to make bricks that are stronger than concrete. *World Architecture*. Retrieved March 7, 2026, from https://sl1nk.com/i54mrbu.

Ward, G., & Khan, K. (2023, September 25). Meet the Kenyan woman turning plastics into bricks. *Euronews*. Retrieved March 7, 2026, from https://l1nq.com/0k11s2f.

Ward, G., & Khan, K. (2023, September 25). Meet the Kenyan woman turning plastics into bricks. *Euronews*. Retrieved March 7, 2026, from https://l1nq.com/pdgqzrx.

Whitehead, J. (2021, June 7). Cupffee: The coffee cup you can eat. *FoodNavigator*. Retrieved March 7, 2026, from https://l1nq.com/qvk1fdd.

World Bank. (2018). *What a waste 2.0: A global snapshot of solid waste management to 2050. World Bank Group*. https://doi.org/10.1596/978-1-4648-1329-0.

World Bank. (2020). *Stemming the plastics tide in Indonesia: Policy, investments, and research. World Bank Group*. https://hdl.handle.net/10986/34648.

World Bank. (2016). *Enhancing urban resilience: Ghana urban sanitation and solid waste management diagnostic. World Bank Group*. https://l1nq.com/w0vcm1j.

World Bank Group. (2021). *Market study for the Philippines: Plastics circularity opportunities and barriers. World Bank*. https://hdl.handle.net/10986/35295.

Yin, R. K. (2009). *Case study research: Design and methods (Vol. 5)*. Sage.

Zami, M. T. (2025, April 23). Textile giant Bangladesh pushed to recycle more waste. *Thomson Reuters Foundation*. Retrieved March 5, 2024, from https://sl1nk.com/6tn33h5.

Zhang, A., Zhang, C., Munir, H. *et al.* (2025). Circular economy policies in China and Europe: A systematic literature review. *Circ.Econ.Sust. 5*, 5581–5612. https://doi.org/10.1007/s43615-025-00689-y.

Cambridge Elements

Economics of Emerging Markets

About the Series

The aim of this Elements series is to deliver state-of-the-art, comprehensive coverage of the knowledge developed to date, including the dynamics and prospects of these economies, focusing on emerging markets' economics, finance, banking, technology advances, trade, demographic challenges, and their economic relations with the rest of the world, as well as the causal factors and limits of economic policy in these markets.

Cambridge Elements ☰

Economics of Emerging Markets

Elements in the Series

Harnessing Sovereign Wealth Funds in Emerging Economies toward Sustainable Development
Mona Mostafa El-Sholkamy and Mohammad Habibur Rahman

The Emerging Economies under the Dome of the Fourth Industrial Revolution
Mark Esposito and Amit Kapoor

On the Road to Economic Prosperity: The Role of Infrastructure in Ghana
Tuan Anh Luong and Zenas Azuma

Banking Stability and Financial Conglomerates in European Emerging Countries
Pavla Klepková Vodová, Iveta Palečková and Daniel Stavárek

The Paradox of Gender Equality and Economic Outcomes in Sub-Saharan Africa: The Role of Land Rights
Evelyn F. Wamboye

Mobile Banking and Access to Public Services in Bangladesh: Influencing Issues and Factors
M. Kabir Hassan, Jannatul Ferdous and Hasanul Banna

BRICS and the Global Financial Order: Liberalism Contested?
Johannes Petry and Andreas Nölke

Global South Leadership Style: Strategies for Navigating Emerging Economies
Abel Femi Adekola, Mona Pearl, Bruno S. Sergi and Richard Muszynski III

Islamic Finance and Sustainable Development
M. Kabir Hassan, Aishath Muneeza and Rashedul Hasan

Digitalization in Emerging Economies
Mark Esposito, Yusaf Akbar and Frank Campbell

Public-Private Dialogs to Spur Export-led Growth: The Case of Productivity Taskforces in Namibia
Andrés Fortunato and Miguel Angel Santos

Embracing the Circular Economy in Developing Nations: A Pathway to Sustainable Growth and Resilience
Sandeep Goyal, Bruno S. Sergi, Sarthak Kaushish and Priyanka Chaudhry

A full series listing is available at: www.cambridge.org/EEM

Printed in the United Kingdom by TJ Clays Ltd.